MINNIE MAYLOW'S STORY
AND
OTHER TALES
AND
SCENES

JOHN MASEFIELD

✶

MINNIE MAYLOW'S STORY

AND

OTHER TALES

AND

SCENES

✶

LONDON

WILLIAM HEINEMANN LTD

FIRST PUBLISHED 1931

—

PRINTED
IN GREAT BRITAIN
AT THE WINDMILL PRESS

NOTE

THE Tales and Scenes in this volume are copyright. They may not be recited nor performed in public without the licence of the Author or his Agents, the Society of Authors, 11, Gower Street, London, W.C., to whom application should be made.

TO

MY WIFE

I thank the beautiful speakers—

        Chrystabel Ayling
        Betty Bartholomew
        Dulcie Bowie
        Rose Bruford
        Margery Bryce
        Elspeth Coghill
        Nevill Coghill
        Leslie Davey
        Sybil Heriz-Smith
        Hubert Langley
        Judith Masefield
        Amy Rean
        Harold Ripper
        Ronald Watkins
        Penelope Wheeler

who, in the speaking of these tales and scenes,
have deeply delighted me.

                    JOHN MASEFIELD

CONTENTS

PROLOGUE

I AM a pilgrim come from many lands,
With stories gather'd about many fires,
Some, when the moon rose above Asian sands,
Some, when the sun set over English shires.

How often have I told these tales before
To you, the listening pilgrims, who anon
Set out towards the wells you thirsted for
Across the desert, while the planet shone?

Often, perhaps; and often may re-tell,
In distant lands and times, as daylight fails,
When you, the pilgrims, camp beside the well,
And I, the pilgrim, recollect the tales.

MINNIE MAYLOW'S STORY

ONCE (long ago) there was an English King,
Who loved good stories more than anything.

Many a story did the poets tell
To him, who loved their tales and listened well.

But one defect their tales had, that they ended,
Always, at last, the lady was befriended,

The sinner was confounded, lovers blest.
The story's sun went down into the west.

Then the King said, "Would poets could
    contrive
An endless tale, whose heroes do not wive;

A story ever fresh and never done,
Like the august procession of the sun.

Royally watching mortals from the sky,
That sinks, but rises, and can never die."

Then he proclaimed, "It is our royal will
That poets (duly qualified in skill)

Come to our court, and tell an endless tale."
But those who tried it were of no avail.

Their stories lagged enfeebled and then died,
So that in disappointment the King cried,

"Henceforth it shall be death, to any man,
Who comes to court declaring that he can

Tell me an endless tale and fails therein,
It shall be death, like treason, or great sin,

Upon the headsman's block on Tower Hill.
But any poet who shall have the skill

To tell an endless tale shall have for prize
My daughter's hand and half my baronies;

And, when I die, shall have my crown as heir.
Heralds, go forth: proclaim this everywhere."

It was proclaimed, but, when the threat was
    known,
The story-tellers left the court alone,

Even though the princess' beauty was so great
As to tempt any poet to his fate.

Though she was known as Emily the Fair,
Heartsease, and Morning Star, and Golden Hair:

Each story-teller feared to lose his head.
Then the King grieved, for his delight was dead.

No story-teller came with thrilling rhyme
To charm his soul with 'Once upon a time'.

Only his Juggler and the Fool remained:
One he disliked, the other he disdained.

Then silence fell upon the palace hall,
Save for the sentry passing on the wall:

Or some old general coming to report
On army remounts at his frontier fort.

Men with most dreary tales of old attacks,
With half their brains gouged by the battle-axe;

Or ministers with courtesies in their spines,
Or Labour members talking about mines;

Or scarlet admirals, whose breezy tone
Made the King thankful to be left alone.

None who could charm him, as in days of old
The poets with the stories that they told.

And Emily the Fair, with downcast eyes,
Guided the bright silk of her 'broideries.

Loving her father, yet, without offence,
Wishing the loved one might have had more
  sense,

And not be self-condemned to sit like lead,
Dumb by the fire betwixt meat and bed,

Or snarling, as he pokt the burning logs,
"This land of mine is going to the Dogs."

4

One night the porter came before the King,
Saying, "Behold, my lord, a marvellous thing,

Here at your gate a young man brings a tale
That will go on for ever without fail.

He knows the penalty of unsuccess,
His head upon the gate, but none the less

Determines to adventure for the prize."
"Young," said the King. "The young are never
    wise

And all their stories are but washy stuff:
Still, youth demands until it has enough.

This man shall have enough, like all the rest.
Bid him go see the chaplain; it were best

He make his peace before he make his trial."
"He would not take advice, nor yet denial,"

The porter said: "but hungers to begin."
"Checking a fool in folly is not sin,"

The King replied, "so let him come to me:
Put up your night's embroidery, Emily.

A tale-teller has come to show his skill."
Now the dark palace-hall began to fill,

With knights and men-at-arms and palace dames
And pine logs on the fire cast ruddy flames

That made the shadows dance upon the wall.
Then the King rose and said, "Friends, listen all.

A story-teller comes to-night to try
His fortune in a tale that cannot die.

Where is he, porter? Let the lad appear."
A young man at the entrance answered "Here."

And coming forward stood before the King,
Bright as the golden pheasant in the Spring,

Cool as the antlered royal on the crag,
Tense as the racehorse waiting for the flag.

Then the King said, "You doubtless know the
 rules
That hedge our Throne from the attempts of
 fools.

Those who begin and fail in the attempt
Stand self-condemned and none shall be exempt,

Steel lops away the peccant proser's head.
Your person seems unready to be dead."

"Sire," the youth said, "I understand the terms.
I dread no headsman's axe, nor coffin worms,

I venture all things gladly for the stake:—
This fair Princess for whom so many ache.

I do not come for glory nor for land
But as a suitor striving for her hand.

If I succeed, and she will have me . . . well.
If not, come headsman with the burial knell:

And shut me from the presence of her worth.
For the most beautiful princess on earth,

7

I come to tell a story without end."
Then the King answered, "Very well, my friend.

If you can tell a tale that will endure
Daily as sunrise and as season-sure,

This fair Princess and half my land shall be
Yours, now, and all my kingdom after me.

But if you fail, you die: are you content?"
"Yes," the youth said: "the terms are excellent.

If you permit, I will begin my story:—
Our ancient poets, excellent in glory,

Say that of old this England had a King
Who dreaded Famine above everything . . .

Dreaded, lest anywhere, in toft or street,
Subject of his should lack enough to eat,

And he behold his people wanting food.
So, being eager for his country's good,

He swore, on coming to his father's throne,
That, while he ruled, hunger should be unknown

To woman, child or man throughout his realm.
Then being crowned, and settled at the helm,

He called for England's chiefest architect,
Firstly to draw, and after to erect

A granary with cellars, walls and roof
Water proof, tempest proof, and earthquake
    proof.

When this was done he bade his Treasury
Purchase all corn, and fill the granary.

*   *   *

The granary was filled, up to the hatch
With peerless wheat and barley without match.

'Now we are saved,' the King cried, 'from our
    dread
And we can sleep with an untroubled head,

9

And shall not dream of hunger, nor of towns
With all their people starved to skeletons;

With their lips green from biting on the grass.
Men shall forget that ever Famine was.

This grain will last through ten lean years
    together;
Let blight, or smut, or rust, or rainy weather,

Or wind, that lays the blade and earths the ear,
Let them all come, I say: We need not fear;

We have destroyed what has destroyed mankind.'
So, with glad heart, contented in his mind,

He bade them seal the granary hatch with lead.
'Let Famine fall,' he thought, 'we shall be fed.'

But mark, O King, upon how small a point
A mortal craft will shipwreck and disjoint.

In that gigantic granary's topmost wall
One tiny scrap of mortar came to fall,

Leaving a chink that no man's eye could see,
Being aloft where men could never be.

Now, King, this vasty mass of gathered wheat
Sent forth a smell, unknown by man, but sweet

To all the locusts of the world, who flew,
Longing to see where so much eating grew.

So that the skies were dark with locusts flying,
Then for three days men saw the locusts trying

To find some entrance to that shuttered store:
And in the end one lively locust tore

Through that small chink from which the mortar
    fell
And stole away one grain. O King, I tell

Nothing but truth. Another locust came
And struggled through the hole and did the
    same.
And then another locust did the same.

As secretly as sickness in a bone,
So wrought these locusts utterly unknown.

Who could suspect a cranny? Who suspect
The building Guild, the royal Architect?

Unseen as poison breathed in with the breath;
Each of three locusts dealt a corn a death.

Then came a fourth and took a corn and went
Then a fifth locust who was bulky, bent

And almost blocked the chink, but struggled
  through
And took a grain, and a sixth locust, too.

And then a seventh crept into the hole;
And then an eighth; and eighth and seventh stole

Each one a grain, and carried it away
And then a ninth one, having seen the way,

Crept in and took a barleycorn and fled.
The tenth was a king-locust, spotted red.

He took three grains, being of royal blood.
The eleventh took a grain and found it good.

Then the twelfth locust, shining in the sun
Crept in and took a grain. The thirteenth one

Followed and took a corn. The fourteenth came
And took a corn. The fifteenth did the same
And then the sixteenth locust did the same.

And another locust carried off another.
And another locust came, the first one's brother.

He took a corn, and then his brother drew
It through the hole, and took another, too.

And then another locust found the place
And another locust followed him in chase,

And another locust followed close behind
And another locust, hungry as the wind,

Leaped in upon his tracks and took a corn
And a battered locust, who was all forlorn

Lame in one leg, and sorry on the wing,
Came in and took another grain, O King.

Sometimes in hot Septembers one may see
On gray cathedral roofs the wasps in glee

Whirling against the blue sky overhead
From papery nests hung underneath the lead,

So men beheld these locusts, but none guesst
That greed of grain had given them such zest.

There came a black Saturnian one, there came
A stalwart Jovian, with crest of flame.

A glittering, dainty Venus-locust flew
Questing for corn, red Martians followed, too.

Each took a grain, and then, a marvellous sight
A locust bowed with age, whose hair was white,

Thrust to the corn . . ."
           But here the King cried, "Hold.
Boy, by our Father's Corpse down in the mould

Stop this unworthy folly of the flies.
Get to your tale." The young man said, "Be
    wise . . .

Govern your kingdom, Sire, as seems good
But leave a story-teller to his mood.

I tell the tale of what the locusts did.
Another locust crept within and hid,

Under a pile of wheat and took two grains.
And then a locust suffering from pains,

Searched for a peppercorn to warm his marrow:
Then a sow-locust with her twenty farrow

Crept one by one into the chink and stole
And then another locust found the hole,

And crept within and pillaged like the last
And then another locust followed fast.

And then another locust followed soon.
Then one, with wits unsettled by the moon,

15

Strayed crooning through the hole and did the
    same.
And then another, and another came.

And then another and another followed
And soon the space between the bricks was
    hollowed,

So as to hold a locust and a quarter;
And then another locust pressed the mortar.

And then another came and wore it smooth,
And then another came and fleshed his tooth

Right to the bitter kernel of an oat.
Then yet another, with a greedy throat

Came in, and then his cousin, and his aunt."
"Stop!" said the King. The young man said, "I
    can't.

I have to tell my story as it was.
I serve poetic truth, a noble cause.

I will not stop for conqueror or king.
Another locust came upon the wing."

"Silence," the King said. "Silence. Tell me,
    friend,
How soon this locust incident will end?"

"It will not end," the youth said. "It will go
As it has gone for ever. You will know

All that each locust of those millions did,
Give ear, my King." The King said, "Jove
    forbid!"

"It is my tale," the youth said, "and you shall.
I staked my life upon it in this hall,

To tell a story for your prize, and now
Many might think you meant to break your vow.

Let me proceed. Another locust came."
"Young man," the King said, "you have missed
    your aim.

Your story fails, although I grant you clever;
Those locusts could not carry corn for ever.

17

They might have for a year, but in the end
That granary was bare. What then, my friend?"

"Sire," the youth said, "the King who made the
    store,
Filled it again, much fuller than before.

And another locust came and took a corn."
"O readiest story-teller ever born,"

The King cried, "you have conquered; we submit
And, as our Daughter seems rejoic'd at it,

Son, you shall marry Emily the Fair,
Have half my kingdom now, and be my heir.

My heralds shall design you a device,
On a field wavy, semée wheat and rice,

Three locusts proper, bearing each a grain.
Girl, never let him tell that tale again!"

ADAMAS AND EVA

WHILOM there was, dwellyng in Paradys
Our fader Adamas with Eve hys wyf.
They nere not sinful folk in any wys
But angelyk they lived, withouten stryf:
They moughte so have lived all her lyf
Dronk the clene wel withouten Dethe's curse,
But out, allas, al fel as I reherse.

O hellish Sathanas, feend dampnable.
O corsed foule wrecche, soth to say,
Thou wast so wlatsom, so abhominable,
And eke so mordrous without any nay,
Thou didst persuade Eva welaway
To take the greene pomme from the tre
O fatal apple, seed of miserie!

For as hit fel by dominacioun
Of thise derke sterres, as I gesse
Or rede Mars in Opposicioun
To Fortune's brighte sterres, More or Lesse,
Or declinacioun of lukkinesse,

God wot, I nis no more than a babe.
Redith thise clerkes on the Astrolabe.

But so hit fel that Adam is ygo
Out of thys garden for a day or twey,
Him liste se the wilde horses go
Thise litel prety Centaures, soth to sey,
So forth he goth, though Eva said him nay
He careth never a del, forth is he went.
Now Sathanas, let launch thy fel intent.

This corsed wrecche, I mene this Sathanas,
Upon his bely sobtilely doth crawl
Into thys garden on the grene gras
Ther as the thikke hegge has i-fal,
Or els a mous had eten through the wal
And left an hole: he on his bely crepith
To the grene bour thereas Eva slepith.

O Judas of dissimulacioun,
O false Ganelon of evil lukke,
Fly, sparwe, fly, with informacioun,
Beth Adam 'ware the feend is with hys chukke:
O pypen, blisful goos, o quakke dukke,
Warn sely Eva sleeping in the bour
Ther comth this false corsed tregetour.

But as thys Cato saith in Scipioun,
In his old boke that thise clerkes rede,
"Though all men shryken Morder in the toun
What botes it if the wrecche have done the deed?"
The woful cors, forblodied, skarlet-reed,
Gettith no gost, for al they cry Allas.
Now comth this Sathanas where Eva was.

O sely Eva, moder of us al,
Thou wast to nice and grene, ye, God woot,
The rede apple round as is a bal
Goth doun the sclendre golet of thy throot;
Thou ettist it when thou was tolde noot . . .
Wepe, Adam, wepe, thy wyf has lost hir sense,
Sewith thy napron, farewel innocence.

For ye han herd how Adamas and Eve
For apple-take were chased our of hir bour,
Where the swete birdis sang in the grene leve
They might not stop a minute ne an hour.
Their salte teres wetted many a flour;
Hem listed nat to wenden wel away,
But out they went, ther nis namore to say.

SON OF ADAM

ONCE on a time there was a lusty Lion
Just come of age, within the Libyan desert,
A handsome he, all shiny with manly beauty.

So on his coming-of-age-day out he went
Forth from his father's palace, caring no straw
For how his Mother beggd him to be careful:
For "Oh," she cried, out of the palace turret,
"Beware, my lovely boy, of Son of Adam.
Of all the dangerous deadly beasts of Earth,
He is the dangerousest and the deadliest."

This shiny Lion, full of beauty of youth,
Went to the drinking-pools where the gazelles
    went,
But not to seek gazelles. Into the water
He peered a long, long time at his reflection,
And smiled and said: "Perhaps not beautiful,
But oh, how interesting and how virile.
Let Son of Adam come here: only let him."

Then, rising up, he pac't into the desert
Shewing his teeth, lashing his flank with his tail,
And with deep coughing roars calling aloud
"Come, Son of Adam, with your deadly danger."

And lo, out of the air there came a stranger,
A grey bird ghastly, with all tail feathers gone,
Part pluckt, part moulted, altogether batterd.

"What Animal are you?" the Lion askt it.

"I'm a Goose Animal," the creature answerd.
"And I am running away from Son of Adam
Who longs to cook and eat me: he has ravisht
My feathers, as you see: it is his custom
To eat us geese with apple sauce and sages;
Our feathers stuff his beds, our grease, out-
    melted,

He rubs upon his skin to make him shiny.
He is a deadly thing, the Son of Adam."

The Lion answer'd: "Leave the matter to Me.
Myself will deal with him and see you righted."

He pac't a little further upon his way
And lo, another creature, witherd and gray,
Came hobbling, stumbling, ribbed and shoulder-
    sorry
A lop-eared, pondering thing, clever, perverse.

"What Animal are you?" the Lion askt it.

"I am a Donkey Animal," it answerd.
"And I am running away from Son of Adam.
Who bangs me with a stick and makes me labour
Dragging the load of barley sacks to market,
Beatings and kicks and curses are my portion,
The chaff the horses leave, the hay the cows leave,
The meal the pigs refuse, and autumn wind-falls:
These, and, sometimes, a happy dream of carrots.
A dream, I say, a vision, that on waking
Fades to an empty crib with the rain dripping.

Such is my life, but even when pale Death comes
To end my life of sorrows and release me
Still Son of Adam comes, he takes my skin off
And moulds it into what he knows as vellum
On which his devilish deep ones write their deeds.
Dangerous are the deeds of Son of Adam."

"Leave him to me, my friend," the Lion answerd,
"Myself will deal with him and see you righted."

Onwards he pac't, engrosst in his importance,
And as he felt the wiseness of his wisdom,
Lo, coming thither was another creature
A little like the Donkey in his feature
But shorter in the ear and sadder-looking
The ribs more staring and the knees more broken
Such as a cats'-meat man would rub his hands at.

"What Animal are *you?*" the Lion askt it.

"I am a Pack-Horse Animal," it answered.
"And I am running away from Son of Adam.
Deadly and dangerous is Son of Adam:
He makes my life a burden beyond bearing,
With ploughing, harrowing and homing harvest,
Taking the sacks to mill, turning the mill-stone,
Then dragging back the flour to the baker.
And always being ridden, having my jaw jabb'd
With snatchings on the bit and "Back there, will
        you."
And always getting saddle-galls and spavins
And curby hocks and colic and the staggers.

And for my food, to give me strength to labour
I ask you what, and Echo answers with me.
Chaff that a sailor would reject in biscuit;
Hay that a politician would not purchase
During a war, and corn the forage merchants
Could not dispose of, even to a general.
And in the green time, in the happy summer,
When the pink clover blossoms in the hayfield,
And all beasts banquet, never think that I do,
Not with a Son of Adam for a master
I snatch a dusty mouthful from the roadside
The while I drag the hayload to the hayrick
And even then am struck, and Son of Adam
Cries 'You're not here to gormandize but labour.
Pull up, now, to your collar; pull, you cab-horse.'

And even when I perish, Son of Adam
Makes profit of me, selling me to kennels
To boil with barley into broth for foxhounds,
And others boil my horny hoofs for jelly
And sell my flesh for cats'-meat or for sausage;
Unhappy Pack-Horse, deadly Son of Adam."

"Leave him to me, my friend," the Lion answerd.
"Myself will deal with him and see you righted."

So, pacing on, he mus'd, "In after ages
These paltry beasts will raise a temple to me,
The Lion of all Lions of all Lions
Loud roaring vanquisher of Son of Adam,
Where is this Son of Adam? Let me see him."

And as he spoke, behold, coming towards him,
There was a Something of a mildewed aspect
So sorrowful, so furless and so feeble
That it was doubtful what it could be reckon'd;
Whether an Animal or only Nightmare.

It had no teeth to speak of, and no talons,
No fur upon its head, but moulted baldness,
Two wretched legs it had, and one a lame one,
A coat all ragged, shewing rags beneath it.
Across its back was slung a builder's wallet
And on its shoulders, staggeringly, it bore
A load of planks and also an iron door.

And seeing it, at first, the Lion doubted
Whether to stoop to speak to such a creature.
Then with extreme misliking and disfavour
He askt the thing: "What Animal are you
    then?"

The creature, putting down his burdens, panted
And toucht his brow, and said, "To tell the truth,
    sir,
I am a Builder Animal, so please you.
And I am running away from Son of Adam,
Because I can't agree with Son of Adam.
And why? Because this Son of Adam asks me
To build at things I cannot reckon building.
They are not building, no, but jerry-building,
These bungalows in ribbons down a roadside,
These cottages constructed by the Council,
Workers like me can't reckon them as building.
Give me to build at building that *is* building;
One of these towers like a minaret now
Or pyramid all pointed for a Pharaoh . . .

But tripe, not taste, is Son of Adam's fancy.
No use to talk to him of architecture
Besides he wants no workers, no, but wage-
    slaves
That he can grind to do his deeds of darkness.
I tell him plain I'll do no jerry-building . . .
Since Builder-Animals must die like others,
I say 'Die building palaces not pigsties.'
So here I come, to build a palace *and* die."
Salt tears were glistening in the Builder's eye.

"I come," he said, "prepard to build a palace
For him they call the King of Beasts, the Monarch
Of all live things, the Conqueror and Captain
The Emperor of Animals, The Leopard."

"Leopard?" the Lion said, "You are mistaken.
The Leopard is not Emperor nor Captain,
Nor Conqueror, nor Monarch; he is nothing . . .
The certain spotty grace that we accord him
He shares with currant dumplings and hyænas . . .
And as for King, he's less a King than you are.
Lions have palaces and leopards lairs, sir . . .
And that if Lions choose. I am a Lion . . .
Build me a palace: talk no more of Leopards . . .
    For by the Lion Sun who ranges Heaven
Tossing his mane of fire from his shoulders,
To talk of Leopards in such terms is treason."

"Forgive me my mistake, sir," said the Builder.
"It comes from all that Son of Adam taught me.
Leopards indeed! Indeed I see my error,
Seeing a royal Lion like yourself, sir,
(That is, as far as I can see, from dazzle).
O what great joy and rapture and promotion
For this poor wage slave 'scapt from Son of Adam

To build a palace for a Royal Lion
A Conqueror and Emperor and Sultan.
To think that with these plankings and this
    hammer
These hands will build a palace for your King-
    ship
To see your smiles and echo with your singing
And gleam with the reflection of your beauty.
For, Sir, when I beheld your beauty coming
I thought, 'This is some planet or some angel.'
And now, to think I am to build your palace.
O happy Builder-Animal, thrice happy:
O lucky nails, O blessed plank and hammer."

And as he spoke, he built a little palace
Then turnd it upside down, and through the
    bottom
Drove four and five inch nails, so that the points
    stuck
Up, through the floors, and each one pointing
    inward.

"Why drive the nails like that?" the Lion askt
    him.

"In royal palaces we always put them,"
The builder said, "It is the royal hall mark.
The palace is now ready, if it please you.
Will you walk in?"

"It is not very big," the Lion answerd.
"There's lots of room inside, I do assure you,"
The Builder said, "As sweet a little palace
Ay, and as roomy as a King could look for.
Just step inside and see it for yourself, sir."

So stooping down the Lion crawled within it,
And instantly the Builder clapped the door to,
The iron door, and lockt it with a padlock.
Then went away, but soon returned rejoicing
Riding the Donkey Animal, and plucking
The Goose for dinner, while he drove the Pack
    Horse.

He halted there, and hove the Lion palace
The Lion still inside, onto the Pack Horse
And drove him to the Sultan, where he sold him.

THE LOVE GIFT

In King Marc's palace at the valley-head
All seem'd in happiness: Isolt the Queen
And Marc the King were lovers newly wed;
Brangwen, the maiden, watcht them with soft
    eyes;
Tristan would pluck his harp-strings till they
    pled
To all hearts there, and April flourisht green.
Men said, "Our kingdom becomes Paradise."

But Tristan and the Queen were lovers sworn
Both having drunk the love-drink meant for
    Marc.
Brangwen in bitter anguish went forlorn,
Loving the King: she, too, had drunk the dram,
Had played the Queen that marriage night till
    morn,
And lived upon her memory of the dark.
These souls, like petals in a mill-race swam.

It fell that Marc, upon Midsummer Eve,
Went to the holy hill above the wood
And saw the moon steal slowly up and cleave
The white, still clouds that glitterd as she came.
And lo, he saw the forest-goddess leave
The aged Oak of Watching that there stood;
She sped to him, and called him by his name.

She was a mighty lady crowned with oak
In its young green, with oak-apple; she held
In her left hand a spear clutcht to her cloak,
Her marvellous hair was gathered to her head.
Her sandals were bright fire without smoke.
Her robe was of fresh beechen leaves all stell'd
With hawthorn blossom that never would be
    dead.

Antlers she bore, and from her leafy dress
Peer'd squirrels' eyes intelligencing quick
All things that happen'd with all sudden-ness.
The swiftness of the forest life was hers
All, from the ousel running 'neath the cress
To soft-foot stags that never snap the stick;
Her voice was as the forest when it stirs.

"King Marc," she said, "Since you have
    honour'd me
At all times, having kept this holy copse
From hunting horn and hound forever free,
Nor let the woodmen's axes lop and split
The branches of my oaken dwelling-tree,
Where falcons nest and the red squirrel hops,
Now you shall joy in my reward for it.

"I have three gifts to offer to your choice:
Wisdom and Power and Immortality,
Wisdom that makes the spinning stars rejoice;
Power that makes the singing stars to spin;
And last, that Death shall never still your voice,
Eternal Living, Marc, from Death set free.
Which shall I give you? you shall choose: begin.

"Each of the three gifts you may give away
But must not share: I cannot help you choose:—
Each is a glory wrested from the clay
By spirit striving against mortal odds
To hive a little sunlight from the day.
Each is a splendour for immortal use,
Each, being had, will make you like the gods."

She waited, while Marc pondered which to
    take
Of those three glowing fruits the goddess had.
Rejecting any would be such mistake
But this he thought: "Since any may be given,
Which were the loveliest gift for me to make
To my beloved Queen, to make her glad?
Which would my Isolt love, my bird of
    Heaven?"

And thought "The gift of Immortality
Would be the loveliest gift, it would ensure
That Death would spare that living ecstasy,
That April, at whose passing the grass springs;
Death should be powerless on such as she;
That White Rose of Midsummer should endure,
Bringing forever the beauty that she brings . . .

"Therefore," (he told the goddess) "I will
    choose
Immortal Life of what you offer here
Healing to every cut, balm to each bruise,
Life, flowing in wherever fever is,
Life, the advancing knight who cannot lose,
Life, that is enemy to death and fear,
Life, that brings vision to the mind amiss."

The goddess gave the central glowing fruit,
"This gives immortal life to whomso eats,"
She said, "It grows upon a deathless root
Men see it glimmer if they give their lives.
Breath cannot falter nor the pulse be mute
Of whomso swallows its exciting sweets.
Eat and be quit of all that Death contrives:

Or give (you may not share) if give you must . . .
Only a god's gift should not lightly pass
At greedy bidding from a mortal lust.
God chooses the recipients of his gifts,
As earthly kings their messengers of trust,
The golden vessels not the things of brass,
Not clay that crumbles nor the sand that
      shifts."

Then she was gone as stilly as the moon
Creeps into mist: not any hazel stirrd.
Marc lookt upon the goddess' glowing boon:—
A quince, like living ember to the sight;
Of intense tint, but ever changing soon,
As gorget jewels on the humming-bird;
Now drawing to itself, now giving, light.

Then hastening back to palace, Marc repair'd
Straight to the Queen and cry'd "Isolt, my own,
I bring you here Life's very essence bared.
Accept the fruit of immortality;
The spirit powers forbid it to be shared;
Its excellence must be for you alone,
Life at its fullest, for eternity.

"The goddess gave this wonder even now
And said: 'The Eater cannot taste of Death,'
This apple grew on an immortal bough
Whose roots are thrusted in eternal things.
Beloved, with this gift I Thee endow,
Eat, my beloved, that your blood and breath
May be exempt from mortal sorrowings.

"And be, forever, beauty, as they are
Now, to myself, O treasure of the West.
My joy, my Morning and my Evening Star,
I have so long'd for such a gift to give . . .
The winds will blow my perisht dust afar
This dust that loves you and that you have
        blest.
What matters that, beloved: you will live."

Then Isolt took the Fruit of Life and said
"Marc, you were ever generous, to the soul;
I take this precious gift that you have made.
But for the eating of this living fruit . . .
That is a question to be deeply weigh'd.
How beautiful it is . . . like glowing coal . . .
Ask me not what I purpose, but be mute

"About it: it were better if we both
Kept silence about this most marvellous gift.
My husband, ever since we plighted troth
You have been royal to me, gift and thought.
I who have profited have suffered sloth
To check the gratitude that should be swift
And generous as the gift, and as unsought."

She bowed her lips upon the fruit and went.
That following afternoon at milking time
When all the palace hinds were up the bent
(Save the smiths shoeing and the men at mill)
She stole into the gallery and lent
Over the rail, and softly sang a rhyme,
And Tristan came at call to know her will.

"Tristan," she said, "My heart's beloved friend,
This fire-glowing fruit that has been given,
Gives to the Eater Life without an end.
I cannot share it; but I cannot eat
Taking a joy I cannot give nor lend
To you, beloved soul, my earthly Heaven.
Take it from me, and be immortal, sweet.

"For then I shall be happy, knowing this
'My Tristan is alive, through love of mine.'
Out of our loving and the joy it is
I give this golden apple of the sun;
Beloved, take it, though it once was his . . .
Marc's . . . it is yours, I kiss it for a sign,
Kiss it for my sake, my beloved one."

So Tristan took the fruit, and as he took
An aged crone beside the fire awoke
In the dark settle in the chimney nook,
And whimper'd; "Ai, my little grandchild's
        late,
And I'm forgotten being palsy-strook;
My breath is shocking and my heart is broke."
Tristan slipt sidelong thence and out at gate.

But being by himself he thought, "Alack,
I cannot take the gift that Marc has given
(Doubtless with passion), I must give it back.
How could I live forever without her?
We are two wild-duck in a single track
Bound to a mere whose reeds are tempest driven
But we are utterly one amid the stir."

So, when he next met Isolt in the hall,
He said: "I cannot keep your precious gift.
We are each other's, let us share in all,
Living or dying, O beloved heart.
Love is most royal, without self, or thrift,
Or wisdom, or concern for what may fall,
Beyond the longing for the counterpart.

"But Isolt, sweet, when first we plotted here
We trickt King Marc, that on his marriage
      night
He drank the philtre that makes people dear,
With Brangwen, not with you: and that offence
Leaves Brangwen sorrowing in love, and drear
With miseries of shame: it would be right
To give this fruit to her in recompense.

"But I refuse a life you cannot share:—
Therefore let Brangwen eat the fruit and live,"
Isolt agreed and calling Brangwen there
They gave the fruit to her, and Brangwen took.
Brangwen the sweet-faced woman with brown
      hair;
Eternal life, but peace they could not give
To her whom Love's devouring fever shook.

All day the gentle Brangwen ponder'd long
Trying to dare, but checkt by shame-facedness,
Then Love, which ever ventures and is strong
Drove her to presence of King Marc to speak.
"O King," she said, "Forgive me if I wrong
Custom or rule in daring to address
Your Majesty uncall'd: I do not seek

"Aught for myself, but humbly offer you
This fruit which makes immortal him who eats
Immortal, as the shining retinue
Of bringers of the Light of God to earth.
All sickness flesh of mortal ever knew
Fades from the eater of these living sweets.
It is for you: man cannot share its worth."

41

Then Marc, in taking Brangwen's gift, was sure
That Isolt had betray'd him to the full,
Loving another someone beyond cure.
He said, "I thank you, Brangwen, for this gift.
Life is a precious boon, if Love endure.
This way and that the angry passions pull;
Many are eager that the end be swift.

"I shall remember that you gave this thing,
And how you gave it, and be ever proud
That subject has so reckon'd of her King."
Then carrying the gift he left the hall
And anguish from the poison of the sting
Wrought in him till he wept with forehead
　　bow'd
Nor heeded whither he was bent at all.

But at the last, he sat beside a brook
And lo, beyond, a little seven year lad
Was weeping with such grief his body shook
Choking with sobs and moaning in between
That Marc, remembering childish sorrows,
　　took
Pity, and askt, what misery he had?
What bitterness had happt to cut so keen?

Then the child answer'd "Mother's going to die,
So Doctor says, of weakness; when she's dead
Bran says that she'll be somewhere in the sky
Where she can never talk to us, nor see.
And Father beats when Mother isn't by,
When drunk, he's beaten me until I've bled.
But Mother's kind: she makes him let us be."

"But, Courage," said King Marc, "and lead me,
        straight,
To where your Mother lies;" then, being brought,
He paused beside the broken cottage-gate
And said, "Go swiftly: make your Mother eat
This Fruit of Living ere it be too late."
The lad ran to the cottage swift as thought.
And laughter follow'd after, that was sweet.

Then the King turned for home, no longer blest,
No longer home, but now the tragic place
Of passionate love's betrayal manifest.
But deeper sorrows than his own were bare,
The inmost ache within the mortal breast,
The pitiful child's crying of the race
For comfort of a soul no longer there.

TRISTAN'S SINGING

PART I

WHEN Isolt quarrell'd with her Tristan there
In the green forest, and returnd to Marc,
Tristan was in the uttermost despair
And fled into the wilds and livd on bark
And found a cavern, once a hermit's lair,
And dwell'd there raving for that lovely
    thing
Gone from him, back to Cornwall and her
    King.

And in his madman's rage, he fashion'd
    bows,
And pointed arrows in the flame, and slew
The red stags of the mountain and their does,
The wolves of the mid-forest and their crew;
He killd, and flung their bodies to the crows,
But took their skins, and pricking with a
    thorn
Wrote on them in his blood his love forlorn.

44

Then, shrieking like the she-wolf gaunt and dire,
He would run raging like a fiend in hell,
Thro' berry-bramble, gorse and forest-fire,
Hunted by love remember'd but too well;
Love gone and living torment of desire:
Then dropping wretched he would rock with
    pain
Weeping for Isolt gone to Marc again.

Thus in a madman's misery he dwell'd
More than a year, then, on a summer night,
He wander'd from his cavern and beheld
The moon in heaven beautiful with light,
And saw the glowing dog-rose many-stell'd,
And joy return'd to him: he wept that things
So beautiful should bless this world of stings.

And as he wept, his spirit was aware
Of joy within him, lightening his mind
To marvels that had lain un-notic't there;
Custom had made him deaf and passion blind.
But now the universe was riven bare,
The very grass was singing from the ground,
The life within him carroll'd at the sound.

45

The sallow clover-clusters ting'd with red
Were rooted in immortal life and spoke
Of earth and living beauty, wine and bread,
That yet are starry in their mortal yoke;
The hairy and dark-crimson basil shed
Wisdom and peace: a moth with jewell'd eyes
Percht on his hand and sang of Paradise.

And all the glittering dusts upon his wings
Expanded and contracted singing too
Their unison and joy as living things,
The unison and joy that Tristan knew.
Life flow'd within him from eternal springs.
"O Heaven," he cry'd, "I am so gulft in bliss
Burn me away and let me live in this."

But, in his joy, a flash of sorrow came:
"This, being dream, will vanish with the night."
But lo, the morning toucht the East with flame
The forest tree-tops shiver'd and grew bright
Cocks from the little tofts without a name
Cried, and the blackbirds leapt out from the
    thorn
Intenser rapture came with day new-born.

For every waking bird and opening flower
And leaf upon the tree and four-foot beast
Cried out his exaltation in the hour
And brighter and still brighter grew the East
Then the great Sun strode up into his tower
And lookt and laught upon this world of men
This world of joy for all was singing then.

Then, from the forest of old, lichen'd oak
That had so often bow'd before the blast,
Leaf-crown'd immortals in procession broke;
Tristan beheld the spirits who outlast
Men, ravens, trees; they smil'd on him, they
    spoke
Those spirits of the waters and the woods,
Whose presence sanctifies the solitudes.

Brown-limb'd and starry-ey'd the Queens of hills
And Kings of glens came, and the Nymphs who
    rule
Brooks, lipping pastures glad with daffodils,
Or water from the chalk up-bubbling cool;
And spirits of the Peace whose beauty fills
Shy places, that the comer kneels in pray'r
That the eternal felt may bless him there.

And lesser spirits, lovely or austere,
Came from the summer bracken and the heather,
The speedwell, harebell and the mouse's ear
And water-guarding reeds with tossing feather
And fox-gloves, that the humble-bee holds dear
All these he saw, all Summer's queens and kings,
Followed by mortal troops of forest-things.

The red-tongue-lolling wolves out of the rocks;
Badgers that root the wasp-nests and the bees;
The kindreds of the poultry-murdering fox;
Stoats from the barren, squirrels from the trees;
And solitary birds and birds in flocks,
Curlews, and little snipe that in the spring
Make heaven noisy with their whinnying.

And there were otters from the mere, and voles
Out of the brook, still nibbling at the cress,
The herons who stand fishing in the shoals
Watching the shadows in the glassiness;
And Kingfishers as bright as blazing coals
Burning blue skimmings where the minnows
        rise
And glittering wing'd green-gleaming dragon-
        flies.

All these went pressing up the Ancient Way
And Tristan follow'd, for a Summer King
Said, "Follow, Tristan; all rejoice to-day,
The lost make merry and the broken sing."
Within the rampart on the hill-top lay
A shelterd field, stone-mossy, scantly grasst,
To this those singers and rejoicers passt.

There they form'd circle, but as waiting still
For something greater that should crown the
      hour;
Joy made the spirit within Tristan thrill
Rapture was his again and peace and power
And all were singing on the holy hill
Bird, beast and spirit, grass and mossy stone,
Joy, yet foretelling greater joy unknown.

And then upon the summit of the year
So burning blue, so crooning with the dove,
Nature herself swept thither with her spear
Nature the naked swiftness, fierce as love,
With mad eyes full of lightning, striking fear,
Hawk-wing'd she was, wing-footed, antler-
      helm'd,
Compact of joy that drew and overwhelm'd.

"Spirits and subject creatures all," she cry'd,
"In this mid-summer hour the ruling sun
Sends rapture into every heart, full tide,
Even now his glory quickens every one.
Sing for mid summer and the full year's pride
And sunlight flooding." At her word they sang
Bird, beast and spirit till the forest rang.

Then Tristan, leaping to her, caught her hand,
And cry'd, "O passionate swiftness, strike and
        kill . . .
I cannot care, being so sown with sand,
But, lovely fierceness, first declare your will;
Null me to dust, but let me understand . . .
What are you, fiery beast or goddess? Tell."
Then Nature's voice made answer like a bell.

"I am so swift, that mortals think me slow;
I am so patient, mortals think me dead;
I am too little for men's eyes to know,
Too vast for what I blazon to be read;
Too jubilant with energy for woe;
Too truthful in my justice to be fierce.
All men must suffer, or annul, my curse.

But you, forsaken soul, by passion burn'd
Into one hunger, being daft and driven,
Bitten by watch-dogs, outcast, outlawed, spurn'd,
To mortal nothingness, shall now have Heaven."
Then Nature told him all and Tristan learn'd.
The tale of Changing, never young nor old,
Dust into man and angel, clay to gold.

Then, having told, she sped, and Tristan went
Back to his cave, but trembling with such
        peace
As made his spirit seem omnipotent . . .
He wrote what Nature told, he could not cease
Though the moon rose, and southt, and west-
        ward leant
And morning stars beheld him as he wrought
Burnt into beauty by consuming thought.

All summer long, from day dawn until night,
The glory of the poem kept him glad,
So that he heeded neither wet nor bright.
Nor the rank chitch, the only meat he had
But beauty well'd from out him in delight
As from the hollow in the chalk the cool
Water comes bubbling to the sunny pool.

Till, when the summer waned and leaves were
    dying
To brown and red, and evening mists were chill,
And yellow crabs had fallen and were lying,
And morning frosts were white upon the hill
And heaven sighd with flocks of migrants flying
On Summer's heel, Tristan arose and said
"Isolt must hear these poems I have made."

So forth he went, a ragged, starving thing
Gaunt as a famine, staring as an owl,
His matty hair and beard like tangled string
His body burnt like brick, his tatters foul.
On Severn bank he heard a church-bell ring
For the first time for months, the sound of
    man.
Then in the dusk an evening hymn began.

Then, lowing as they loiter'd home, the cows
Came swaying up the lane before a hind
Who whistled ballads of the milking house,
And tears of very joy made Tristan blind.
His living soul was come out of its drowse
Of love and madness, he was Man again,
Who had been mad as any fiend in pain.

Southward he went, until, behold, ahead
The river and the palace of the King,
The courtyard and the staghounds being fed,
And horses on the cobbles clattering
And Isolt, too, and Marc, like lovers wed
That morning, there together, entering in
After their gallop on the windy whin.

He knew them, but none present recognized
Himself, the wreck with bracken in his beard,
Him the dogs barkt at and the cats despised
And women shrank from and the children
          fear'd.
The porters markt him closely and surmized
He came for scraps, they watcht he did not steal
A bone from any stag-hound for his meal.

Then Kai, the steward, flaunted to the gate
To bid the porters close it on the throng;
And, seeing Tristan, askt, "Why do you wait?
You, dirty gangrel? Off where you belong."
And Tristan said "I come to supplicate
Leave to approach Queen Isolt, and to sing
One poem to her from this pack I bring."

Kai lookt upon the written skins, and frown'd
And said "But that His Majesty has bidden
That poets shall find Cornwall friendly ground,
Such skins as these should go upon the midden,
And you, yourself, be hunted by the hound
Over the border . . .   I will take your pack
In, to King Marc. Await my coming back."

Soon he return'd and said "The King has
    glanc't
At some of all this scribble: your request
To see the Queen cannot be countenanc't.
She sees no lazar smelling of the pest.
The prospects of your verse might be enhanc't
Were yourself cleaner; but the King, ev'n so
Dislikes it. Take your rubbish. Kindly go."

Marc passt upon the instant and said: "Stay,
You Severn poet, though I cannot care
For what you write, you must not go away
From this my palace, guerdonless and bare,
Give him a cloak and wine and victuals, Kai;
And for your journey westward, take this
    purse."
Then Tristan flung it from him with a curse.

"No, Marc," he said, "I am Tristan, come again
To win back Isolt to me if I can.
Let Isolt tell me if I come in vain.
Let Isolt choose between us, man and man."
"Tristan," Marc said, "I vow'd you should be
      slain:
Hunted and torn to pieces by the hounds
If you were seen within my Kingdom's bounds.

You have wrought harm enough in Isolt's life;
You have disgrac't her, you have brought her pain.
She has renounc't you and is now my wife.
You shall not look upon her face again.
If you attempt it, boy, the hangman's knife
Shall have you into quarters in the yard.
Now you shall leave this Kingdom under guard."

Then the guards, closing on him, dragg'd him
      thence,
Bound him, and flung him in a cart, and drove
Over the frontier to the forest dense
Where slink and savage wild wolves us'd to rove.
Then, flogging him, they left him without sense
And so return'd: the rime-frost striking cold
Reviv'd their victim lying on the mould.

PART II

WHEN morning came, he gather'd up the sheaf
Of poems flung beside him: like a deer
That limps into dark covert for relief
Being sore hurt, so Tristan trod the drear
Dark, water-dripping forest full of grief
Not knowing where, but wandering amiss
Towards the camp where Isolt had been his.

And limping on, at dusk he reacht the place
So beautiful when it had held and shrined
Their summer love together, Isolt's grace,
And all the ecstasy of being blind
To all things but the beauty of a face.
Autumn had wrought her change, the bower now
Was sodden grass and leafless hawthorn bough.

There, with a flint and rags, he lighted fire
And burn'd his poems, all, except the last
That was the song of Nature and Desire,
And of Eternity and Time long past;
Of Doing, Good and Ill, and of its Hire
That never sleeps, but waits, and has its Turn;
This, being Isolt's song, he could not burn.

Daylong he crooned it until even-fall,
Praying for Death to come to give him peace;
And Autumn chill'd, until the oak trees tall
Had droppt the last brown shred of summer's
    fleece,
Then the snug dormouse curld into a ball
Deep under knotty roots in nibbled wool
And silent-footed snow came beautiful.

All winter-long he wander'd, living hard,
On roots and dulse and mussels of the rock
And grain forgotten at the thrashing-yard
And barley-porridge that the fattening stock
Left (or the upland swineherd did not guard)
And green cow-parsley thrusting from the
    snow
And other pasture such as thrushes know.

Then Spring began again and at the stir
Of Earth's green fire thrusting into leaf
Again old passion prickt him with the spur
And April's beauty only added grief
April was only beautiful through her,
But rocking in his woe the tune took power
Nature and he were knitted for an hour.

And living beauty ridded his despair
Till joy compelld him to arise and sing
The song that Nature taught him to its air
That pierct like the green fire of the Spring
Clear as a challenge rang his singing there
The rabbit-bucks crept cock-ear'd out of holes
And stags came tip-toe upon velvet soles.

Still louder rang the challenge of the song
The great, white, black-eared cattle rowsd and
        came
The bull's chin chiselling as he lickt his throng
His brooding eyes alight with sullen flame
The stallion, whickering answer, snappt his thong
And ran to hear: and from the marsh the geese
Trumpeted out to birds the end of peace.

And ducks out of the pond, and cock and hen
Flappt and took wing at hearing of the call
Sheep from the moors turnd thither, hogs from
        pen,
Horses at ploughing, hunters in the stall,
And now it arrow'd in the hearts of men
It struck in Isolt's heart the while she wove,
In King Marc's palace, tapestries of love.

And at the sound she said: "That song of power
Is Tristan calling me: I inly know
That here begins the striking of the hour;
The ebbing ends and here begins the flow,
To sweep us on its crest." She left her bower
And caught her horse and galloppt to the cry
That seemed to draw the winds out of the sky.

And in the forest beast and hurrying beast
Throng'd to the singing; birds from bough to
     bough
Flitted like blackbirds to the cherry feast;
Rapine and mating both forgotten now.
There she found Tristan singing, facing East
Ring'd by the birds and beasts that croon'd and
     sway'd.
As Nature's song went ringing down the glade.

Then, flinging from her horse, she passt the throng
And cry'd: "O Tristan, I have come again . . .
Forget that we have wrought each other wrong
We are as one as western wind and rain.
Forget my cruelty and teach your song
And let us sing together, you and I
And be away together in the sky."

And then they sang together until space
And Time were over for them: Dinan's son
Rapt by the song to that enchanted place
Heard their two voices merging into one
And saw the lovers drawing face to face,
Shining with beauty such as seldom shines
On faces, here, where roses have such spines.

And then, lo, they were one, and all was over
Their rags and robes were fall'n and gleaming
    things,
Spirits, a lover wing in wing with lover
Were laughing in the air and spreading wings
Shining like stars and flying like the plover
Laughing aloft and singing and away
Into some Summer knowing no decay.

*   *   *

Men never saw them more, but Dinan's son
Gathered those relics of the fallen gear
And bore them to the Saint within the Dun
Who sent for precious woods and wrought a bier
Inlaid with goldwork gleaming like the sun
And laid the relics on it and with pray'r
For those two lovers' souls displayed them there.

They lie there still within the holy shrine
And lovers sick with loving go to pray:—
"O God of Love, be such love hers and mine
As to touch Life that nothing can decay
And be at one forever and so shine
Singing forever, blessing sorrowing men,
Like these immortal ones, Amen, Amen."

SIMKIN, TOMKIN AND JACK

BEFORE old Tencombe of the Barrows died,
He called his sons, and said, "Simkin, and you,
Tomkin and Jack, I am at Jordanside.
When I have passed the river you shall have
Each one, a thousand pounds, and this thereto,
This farm and downland where the Barrows
 stand;
Share it; all happy virtue is in land."
He died, the three sons carried him to grave.

Then the three sons debated how to spend
Each one, his heritage; first Simkin spoke:
"I'm not for farming, here at the World's End:
The bailiff can do that; myself am fixt
On Science, to attempt some happy stroke
To make synthetic Man's Flesh which will do
Whatever menial jobs we put it to.
Flesh is but hydrogen and carbon mixt."

Then Tomkin spoke: "A beautiful resolve,
And yet less beautiful than what I plan,
I hope to catch the electrons that revolve

Within the excited brains of splendid men
And make an Essence of the Soul of Man
Injecting this will make the silly sane;
The normal splendid: it will kindle brain.
That done, perhaps I'll think of farming then.

Jack said, "And I, who am a Business Man,
Reject your plans, and farming, which will leave
The practisers more poor than they began.
I shall go Citywards to Stocks and Shares
To venture at a profit and achieve.
Then, having money, haply I'll finance
Your Flesh and Spirit ventures, and advance
This farmstead for week-enders with cheap
    fares."

They went to work: then, on a holiday,
Spent at the ruin'd farm, Jack said, "The Press
Mentions our Barrow on the Roman Way,
And quotes the old Wives' Fable that within
There sits a giant in a golden dress.
Let's dig the barrow open to make sure."
"Right," said the brothers, "Practice is the
    cure
For theories of all sorts: let's begin."

So, out upon the Antient Way they drove.
There was the Barrow forty feet aloft;
Beeches were green about it in a grove;
Rabbits had burrowed deep into its sides.
The brothers settled on a site and dofft
Their coats and collars, then their swinging pick
Rang on the scattered flints with little clicks.
Blisters made bubbles on their fingers' hides.

Three days they dug into the barrow's heart
The shepherd on the downland thought them
　　mad
Then, upon sunset, roofing fell apart
The Sun shone in upon a central cave
There sat a mighty Bone Thing, golden-clad
A skeleton, gold-helmeted, who grinn'd
Sitting below the beech-roots and the wind;
Kingly, tho fifteen centuries in the grave.

Then Simkin said "So the tradition's true . . .
Cro-Magnon skull . . ." And Tomkin: "He is
　　big.
Look, on the bone, the markings of the thew" . . .
And Jack, "This gold will speedily be ours.
A happy end to a successful dig."

64

Then Simkin said: "Synthetic flesh would go
Well, on these bones: a looker-on would know
The kind of chap he was, and all his powers."

Then Tomkin said "If you would clothe his
      bones,
I'd squirt Synthetic Spirit in his veins,
Then he would speak, I think, in monotones,
And tell us something precious about dates."
But Jack said "Brothers, after all our pains,
Let's cover him until the morning: then
Have in the Press and Moving-Picture men
And also charge admission at the gates.

But first, our duty is to take the gold,
It is not safe to leave it as it is."
He took the armour, fold on gleaming fold
Leaving the rib-bones open to the air.
He said "Collectors will be mad for this
Authentic armour fetches any price
And no such armour will be offered twice.
To-morrow we'll be famous everywhere."

That night he clamour'd to invite the Press,
Simkin and Tomkin checkt him as they toil'd

Making in test-tubes many a smelling mess,
Or at a wire-end a spitting spark,
Or violet glowings from the wires coil'd.
They met at breakfast-time with amplest store
Simkin had outer husking, Tomkin core;
Jack was by much less cheerful than at dark.

"You know," he said, "this making flesh and
    soul,
Is going far: I'm not a squeamish man . . .
But in the play the Robots took control . . .
Besides, it's witchcraft, which is counted wrong
By every people since the world began.
The Witchcraft Statutes are not yet repealed . . ."
"Rats," Simkin said, "The plough is put to field."
"Bunkum," said Tomkin. "Up, and come along."

So out they went along the dewy grass
Up to the Barrow where the giant sat
Bone upright like the warrior that he was.
Tomkin took off his jacket, rolled his shirt,
Simkin upon the skullbones set his hat.
"Come, Father Noah," Tomkin said, "At last
We'll get authentic datings of the past.
First body, Simkin. Then the Soul with squirt."

So Simkin wrought his wondrous chymic clay.
The figure, like an image made of wax,
Stared listlessly along the antient way.
"You've made him like a warrior," Tomkin said.
"Now for the soul, to stir him in his tracks."
But Jack in terror cried, "No, not the last . . .
This creature is so awful and so vast . . .
If once you give him life he'll smite us dead."

"Rubbish," said Simkin, "If we give him life
It will be elemental in its form;
If fractious you can stick him with a knife.
Go on with Spirit, Tomkin, fill the gland."
"No, no," Jack pleaded, "you will raise a
storm."
"Bosh," Tomkin said. "Now for it . . . Look
at me."
"Mercy," Jack pleaded, "Let me climb a tree
I would not watch it for all English land."

"Get up your tree," said Tomkin, "And be still."
Jack climbed a little beech tree: Tomkin took
Transmitting wires for the vital thrill
To make the giant lively: Simkin helpt.
"When I count Three," said Tomkin, "You can
look.

67   F

One . . . No, the wire's jammed. Two . . .
    There's a short.
Now the thing's working . . . waken up, old
    sport,
Three . . . there she goes." Jack cower'd down
    and yelpt.

And lo, a marvellous thing, the figure stirr'd
It trembled, then its mighty jointings crackt,
Bones grided in their sockets, as they heard.
Then the thing stood upon its feet and breath'd.
Nothing of living man his glory lackt . . .
He strode into the sunlight, facing east,
At every pulse his majesty increast
He stood like light in something glowing
    sheathd.

Then, looking at the Sun, the figure spoke
Meanings, not words: his hearers understood.
Like morning in their minds his meaning broke:
"O Sun that I have worshippt: Sun that brings
The living green upon the wintry wood,
Sun that brings thought into the barren mind,
Sun that puts beauty into hearts unkind,
Lord of all life and Order, King of Kings,

I once more look upon you and obey
The call to Likeness with the Force that sends
Poetry in the shining of the ray
And Wisdom in the summer of your touch.
All Energy and Beauty are your friends
Your fires shout for rapture but confess
A power supreme above their mightiness
Who captains Heaven and many millions such.

I have been buried long and now awake,
I who was Arthur's comrade long ago.
Man is no longer manhood but mistake.
O spirits of the Morning, come like fire
Come, Arthur, from the dead; let trumpets
    blow."
Then, lifting to his mouth his mighty hand,
He cried "Come, comrades to this holy land
O Light breathe Light upon this land's desire."

Once he called thus, and all the trees stood still;
Twice he called thus, and all the air grew tense;
Thrice he cried thus, and over Barrow Hill
A rush came, like the coming-by of birds,
As spirits never seen by commonsense
Gatherd, and gazed, and gleamd upon the view

Waiting, calm-eyed, for orders what to do
From some great trumpet call transcending
    words.

The brothers saw their many colourd wings
Fold, on their breasts: their beauty was so calm
Each spirit seemd a King of many Kings.
They came to carry light to human souls.
None of those victors carried sword, but palm.
The brothers knew that Arthur's comrade's cry
Had called to England lights that cannot die
Beauties and powers wearing aureoles.

And then . . . what then? . . . the warrior's
    figure died.
The body droopt, as all the aged bones
Droppt into dust upon the downland side.
Nothing was there except a chymic mess
The barrow's tumbled earth and scattered stones.
Then the three brothers heard a cry begin
"Open your doors and let the new life in."
And skylarks rose and sang in nothingness.

THE ROSE OF THE WORLD

DARK Eleanor and Henry sat at meat
At Woodstock in the royal hunting-seat.

Eleanor said: "The wind blows bitter chill . . .
Will you go out?" King Henry said, "I will."

Eleanor said: "But on so black a night . . .
Will you still go?" He said, "I take delight . . .

In these wild windy nights with branches swaying
And the wolves howling and the nightmare
        neighing."

She said "May I come, too?" "But no," said he;
"No, for at night, if robbers set on me

I can defend myself . . . I could not you
In the pitch darkness without retinue."

Eleanor said, "Why is it that you go
Thus, and alone?" He said: "You cannot know.

Leave the King's secrets: let the fact suffice;
Duty demands it and I pay the price."

While Henry reacht his sword-belt from the ledge
She pinnd a tassel in his mantle's edge,

A clue of white silk that would glimmer pale
About his ankles as he trod the gale.

*   *   *

Henry went swiftly in the roaring night
Eleanor saw her token glimmer white.

She followed down the hill, along the brook,
Just seeing by the clue the way he took.

He reacht the forest where the hazels sway'd . . .
Her soul was too intent to be afraid.

He pusht within the forest and was gone
But still among the scrub her token shone.

In the blind forest many trackways led
The hazels swayed, the token shewed ahead.

And as she followed she untwin'd a skein
Of silken floss to lead her out again.

The gale roard in the branches: the beasts shook
Not knowing which direction the step took.

Eleanor knew: she followed thro the night
King Henry's mantle with its patch of white.

A long long way she followed: but at last . . .
A clearing in the forest sweetly-grasst

With apple-trees in blossom that the gale
Tore and flung forth; the token glimmerd pale.

Beyond the apple-garth a little house
Stood, shutterd close among the tossing boughs.

Light shone from out the bower window-chinks;
Eleanor crept as cat-like as the lynx.

The white patch lingered at the door: she heard
A signal knock: within doors someone stirr'd.

All stealthily and still as though for sin
The door undid and Henry passt within.

Then the lock turn'd and Eleanor crept near.
In the gale's roaring she could nothing hear.

Yet near the door a fragrance in the air
Told that a red rose had been crumpled there.

Then in the breaking storm a wild moon shew'd
The fashion of that secret wood abode

The windows high: each crevice tightly shut.
Over the lintel-piece a rose was cut . . .

Eleanor crept about as a cat creeps
In evil midnights when the master sleeps.

No dog was there: no sign of life was there,
Save the faint smell of roses in the air;

And hours passt and hurrying showers passt.
Eleanor watcht what fish would come to cast.

Then suddenly, before the East grew gray
The bolt withdrew to let the King away . . .

Eleanor had but time to crouch and hush
Close in the green of a sweet-briar bush

She heard no word, but someone whispered close
In the King's ear, a someone like a rose.

And white arms, with their clinking bangles drew
The King's head downward in a long adieu.

Then the King turn'd and quietly the door
Clos'd, and the house was silent as before.

*　　　*　　　*

Eleanor watcht, but, lo, the patch of white
Was gone, that should have led her through the
　　　night.

Yet following on his steps she saw his frame
Retread in front of her the way he came

And suddenly she saw him halting dead:
His scabbard's end had caught her guiding
　　　thread.

75

She heard him snap it, but she inly knew
He had not guesst the thread to be a clue.

Afterwards Henry hurried, for the day
Came swiftly, now the storm had blown away.

And lo, the beanfield sweet and blackbirds
    waking
Leaping from hedge and setting brambles shak-
    ing,

And Woodstock dim in trees with nothing
    stirring
Save the cats homing after nights of erring.

*   *   *

Eleanor deckt herself in all her pride,
All that had grac't her as King Henry's bride.

"Were you out late?" she askt. He answer'd,
    "No . . .
It was not midnight when we rose to go.

These midnight councils seldom sit for long."
Eleanor humm'd a merry scrap of song.

She went into her turret and undid
Her chest with iron bandings on the lid.

She took a drowsy and a biting draught
And mixt them both and as she mixt she laught

"This is as heavy sleep upon the life . . .
And this is cutting as an Eastern knife,

Together they will still the April grace
Of Mistress White-Arms in the rosy place."

She put the potion in a golden flask,
King Henry's gift, and went upon her task.

King Henry askt her, "Whither are you bound?"
"On charity," she said, "my daily round . . .

The Christian charity I must not spare
To those poor women lying suffering there."

He said, "God bless your charity." And she
Replied "Amen," and went forth quietly.

She visited her sick with bread and wine,
Then searcht the forest for her silken sign.

She found the floss still clinging, leading in.
"The hunt is up," she said, "The hounds begin."

The forest was all thicket, but the lane
To tread, was blazon'd by the silken skein

Though it was dark in covert, her delight
In what her spirit purpost gave her light.

Then lo, the clearing, and the little house
So fair among the blossom'd apple-boughs

And once again her spirit was aware
Of midmost summers' roses present there.

Within the house she heard a woman sing.
Eleanor knockt the signal of the King.

The chain undid, the bolt was drawn, the key
Turn'd, and the door was open'd, it was she . . .

A girl more beautiful than summer's rose
That in the mid June's beauty burns and glows;

A golden lady graced from foot to tress,
With every simpleness and loveliness,

78

Who, in the second when she saw the Queen,
Knew that her Death had come, for what had
        been.

Eleanor like a striking python seized
That golden child and dragged her as she pleased.

"O darling of the King," she said, "Behold . . .
I, who am Queen, have brought this flask of gold,

Also the common hangman and his crew.
I, being royal, give a choice to you.

Either you drink this poison, and so end . . .
Or I will call the hangmen who attend

And they shall strip you naked and so hoot
And beat you to the Woodstock gallows-foot

Where they shall hang you: choose, then,
        sweetest heart."
The girl beheld Death present with his dart.

The present Death with which man cannot strive.
Death that makes beauty be no more alive.

And is so strange the hot blood can but shrink.
"Threaten me not," she said, "For I will drink.

I, too, am royal: and no way remains."
She drank the golden flasket to its drains,

And straight the savage poison in her side
Thrust on her heart-strings that she sank and
    died.

*   *   *

Eleanor dragged the body to the bed
"Lie there and welcome Henry, Golden Head."

Then forth the grim Queen went, and lickt her
    lips
To think of June's bright beauty in eclipse

And Henry going to his love to find
The candle quencht that shone behind the blind.

"He will thrust in, and find her lying cold."
So Henry did and found the flask of gold

And knew the Queen's contrivance in the Death.
That night the Queen cried "Open . . . give me
    breath

Open the window, for I cannot breathe
The golden roses' tendrils wreathe and wreathe

Over my mouth. O who has crusht a rose
The perfume stifles me: unclose, unclose."

They told her that she dream'd; but she replied—
"The roses choke me: open windows wide.

Someone had crusht a white rose or a red . . .
Can you not smell the perfume that is shed?

It comes so close, I cannot breathe the air."
Thenceforward every day and everywhere

The grim Queen cowered from the haunting
        scent
Of roses crusht, of sweet rose-petals blent

Red, white and golden, coming where she trod.
Henry and Eleanor are now with God,

Whose Face is in all Beauty, as I say.
The pure White Nuns took Rosamund away.

Within their Quire they showed for many years
A little chest or scatolin of hers,

Painted with birds, that Henry once had given.
There the White Sisters prayed her into Heaven

That is the rest for lovers: there they wrought
A white-rose tomb for her from loving thought

So that none thought of her, nor ever will
Save as a lovely thing that suffer'd ill.

There every May the grass above her bosom
Is strown with hawthorn bloom and apple-
　　blossom.

And on the wild-rose spray the blackbirds sing
"O Rose of all the World, O lovely thing."

YOUNG JOHN OF CHANCE'S STRETCH

PART I

WHEN Father died, my Mother ran
Our Farm at Chance's like a man.

When I was turn'd eighteen there fell
This venture that I come to tell.

Out cubbing, Mother bruis'd her knee,
(Jumping a gap) against a tree,

So that she could not go to Fair
To buy us a new plough-team there.
She would not trust the bailiff . . . So
"John," said my Mother, "you must go.
Here's fifty pounds in notes. In town
The one safe tavern is The Crown,
Therefore stay there. A Fair-time stranger
Remember's probably a danger . . .
And with a horse to sell, he's worse.
So John, be careful of your purse.
These Fair-time rogues can so persuade
I marvel any girl's a maid.

Only last Fair time, two men came
To Squire's Hall at Wick-on-Tame,
And said they'd come 'to free the tanks.'
The girl (one of these dolls) said 'Thanks,
Come in,' and led them hand in hand
Upstairs to where the cisterns stand.
There one man said 'Now you be gone
Downstairs and turn the water on,
And watch it as it runs away . . .
And, mind: the instant it turns gray
Or brown, call out to me at once.'

So down the silly creature runs
To sink, and turns on all the taps
And watcht, if they'd run wine perhaps.

And up above, the two men rampt
Through every room and then decampt
While she was watching underneath.
Even the Squire's spare false teeth
Were taken: and of course the men
And things were never seen again.

That shows how risky 't is to trust:
Never believe unless you must

And never then about a horse.
But there: you're my wise boy, of course."

I took the money and the trap
I drove to town without mishap
The day before the Fair began.

Many a gilded swing-boat van,
And horse-go-round, with varnisht nags
And bright brass rails and flying flags
And burning furnace shedding glare
Stood by the pavement in the Square
And showmen fitted up the Fair
Heaving with spanners, lamming mawls.

The gipsy-women with bright shawls
And thick brass earrings and big plumes
Hawkt posies made of autumn-blooms
Stolen from gardens on their way.

Towards the closing-in of day
As I was listening to the cries
Of men with pots and dames with pies
My good old Nurse from Tuttocks Rise
Came by: I stoppt and greeted her

And edging outwards from the stir
We stood and talkt by Grocer's door
Of old times over long before,
Three minutes, I suppose, or four.

And while we talkt, a woman stood
Fingering Grocer's poultry food
Close to us, looking at the grain.
She moved away, but came again
And eyed me hard, and entering in
Ordered some hen-food from the bin
And paid and went.
                              I may be wrong
But thinking of it late and long
Both day and night, in hope of solving,
I think she set the ball revolving
That all the game began with her.

About some points I cannot err.
She heard Nurse name me: then she heard
My home, and things that had occur'd,
And what had brought me to the Fair.
And though she stood before me there
Two minutes, in that crowded place
I never really markt her face.

Then, after sauntering up and down
Seeing the sights, I reacht the Crown,
Made sure the nag was snug, and saw
Him happy, fetlock-deep in straw.

The sun was down, the lamps were lighting,
The Fair's noise came like battles fighting:
The Cheap Jack's cries, the songs and shouts,
And brazen patter from the touts
Arose and lifted lad and girl
Into the mad steam-organ's whirl.
It being time, I went to sup.

And at the cheese, the maid came up
And said that someone wanted me.

So, wondering who this could be,
I went into the hall, and there
A girl with two long plaits of hair,
A school-girl, not eleven gone,
Came up and said, "O, Mr. John,
Please, sir, but would you come anon . . .
To see your sister for a minute?"

"Why, girl," I said, "the Devil's in it . . .
I have no sister . . . never had."

She said, "But please, sir, I was bade
To bring you to her, if you'll come."

"But who are you? Whence are you from?"
I askt, and stared upon the child . . .

Her eyes were innocent, she smiled,
She was well dresst, and trim and clean,
"I'm Maggie Hill, from Tuttocks Green,"
She said, "and stopping for the Fair,
With Mrs. Roberts, Market Square."

"Yes, and who sent you here to me?"

"Your sister, Mrs. Peck," said she.

"Where does she live?"
                              "Up Laurence Lane,
At Rector's Close," she said again . . .
"She's Rector's House-keeper at present."

The girl seem'd merry, straight and pleasant.

"All very well, my girl," I said,
"But listen: some mistake's been made.
Who was it you were sent to fetch?"

"Young Mr. John of Chance's Stretch,
Please sir," she said, "lodged at the Crown.
Perhaps if you would just step down
And speak with Mrs. Peck a second
She could explain . . ."

        And I, I reckoned,
That that was simplest.

        "Right," said I.
"Something or someone's gone awry . . .
We'll put it straight, so lead the way."

The West still smoulderd with the day
And Maggie prattled as she led
About the wonders overhead
The flares, the flags, the horses whirling
And pendulum-like swingboats swirling.
We turned up Lawrence Lane and there
An old house jutted, carven fair . . .
The Rector's house as I knew well.

My leader never rang the bell.
She uppt the steps and opend wide
The door for me to pass inside
Then showed me to a little room
Already darkend into gloom
And said "I'll tell them that you're here."

She vanisht down a passage near
And down some stairs.
                           Myself, alone,
Leaned back against the mantel-stone,
Or straining forward strove to see
What Rector's photographs might be . . .
And saw the bare legs and the dates
Of football teams and rowing eights.

The last light of the sunken sun
Gleamd upon silver flagons won
At school or college: in a rack
Some briar pipes gleam'd, cinder'd black;
Then the gleams died: but no-one came
I struck a match and by the flame
Saw Rector's books and college oar.

An owl cried somewhere out of door.
I thought "I'll go, since no-one's coming."
Yet downstairs stealthy speech was humming,
A rapid whisper'd gabble stirrd
Designed not to be overheard
So thinking, "If they don't intend
To come, this joke had better end."
I moved to window.
                           In the sky

A gnat-pursuing bat went by
And from the Church two shuffling crones
Passt by upon the cobble stones.

Then, just as my resolve grew stronger
To wait there in the dark no longer
One came with candle down the hall
And shadows moved along the wall
Gigantic fingers screening light
A woman came, her face dead-white
And great dark rings of eyes: she laid
The candle down: "O John," she said,
"Forgive me: I was so afraid,
I really could not come before."

She turn'd again and shut the door,
And pluckt the window-curtains to.
She said, "O John, I wish you knew
The joy it is to see you here.
And you are wondering, my dear,

Both who I am and all about me
And more than half inclined to doubt me
But if you'll listen, I'll explain.

It starts in a great deal of pain
All over many a year ago,
In ways they never let you know:
And so, may shock you when you hear.

*   *   *

Listen . . . Your Father, John, my dear,
Many long years ago was wed
To my poor Mother, long since dead.
He farmd in Dorset then, and she
Died a year later, bearing me.
You never heard of that? Alas . . .
This photo shows you what she was.

*   *   *

My Father in his grief, gave over
Me, the poor babe who killed his lover,
To Mother's sisters to be reared . . .

*   *   *

Afterwards, Father disappeared
He never knew nor saw again
Me the poor cause of so much pain.
He left the district and the past
Settled at Chance's, and at last
Married your Mother and began
Anew, like every married man.

92

My Aunts would never let us meet.
But Life's a very little street,
And people knock against each other.
Destiny brought me near my Brother
To house-keep for the Rector here.

And like a spy or pioneer
I've been to Chance's, just to see
If Brother John resembled me.
I had not courage to go in.

I never meant to claim my kin . . .
But seeing you alone to-night
I hungered to, and thought I might.
And then I thought, but if I do
He'll disbelieve; he's certain to;
What man would credit such a tale?

Since most refrain who fear to fail,
I did not speak, but let you pass.
Then afterwards I thought, 'Alas . . .
The heart within my bosom cries
To that young Brother with dear eyes . . .
Why did I let him go?'
                          And you . . .
Knew nothing of me: never knew . . .

And then I thought: it isn't sin
Or fault, to tell him we're akin . . .
But still, he may not care to know.
Or else will disbelieve, and so
I wandered to the Church and sought
My Husband out, for what he thought.

My Husband hadn't doubts nor fear.
He said 'Send Maggie round, my dear,
To ask the lad to see you here.'
Maggie 's the neighbour's child: and now
I've told you all the manner how.

And now, my dear, since I have waited
These years for you as things have fated
Now let me hold you close and kiss.

Why, what a man my Brother is . . .
So tall: so powerfully made.
And all boy-modest and afraid.

Now come below: we've supper laid.
My husband's waiting: come to sup."

All full of honey is the cup
And bitter is the morning's taste.

94

She slippt her arm about my waist
And led me to another room,
Lit by a lamp but still in gloom,
Close-curtain'd where a table stood
With glasses, dishes, plates and food,
A loaf, a cheese, and watercress.
And in one wall was a recess
From which a man (with a black beard)
Holding a jug of wine appeard.

"This is my husband, John," said she.
He took my hand and welcom'd me.

Somehow I didn't like his eyes.

"Have you got over your surprise
At hearing you'd a sister here?"
He askt; "Come, sit, and make good cheer;
But drink, first, to the happy meeting.
Come, drink it to the dregs, no cheating,
It's only claret, mulled. Come, Ann . . .
This John of yours is grown a man . . .
Here's your glass, Ann; here's yours, here's
    mine."

He leaned across and poured the wine.
And smiled, our glasses clinkt, we drank.

Then surging billows rank on rank
Rose somehow out of wall and table
And all the room became unstable
And hummed a tune which droned and rose
And flooded as a river flows.
And I, within it, was as dead
Lapped within rising swathes of red
Thinking "This is great bliss . . . great bliss . . ."

I know not what the next thing is.
I was turned endlong, lifted, hauled
Up-ended, held, supported, mauled,
Why, where or how I had no notion
Save that there somehow was an ocean
Of great red surging waves about.

But somehow someone got me out
To darkness and the open air
And wheeled me in a barrow there
Then tipped me, but I didn't care
Having such glory in my mind

Watching the surges wave and wind.
Then all was dumb: then all was blind.

*   *   *

From vasty distance and with pain
I came to consciousness again.
I wondered at the dark and cold
And why I lay upon the mould,
And why the sky was over me.
Then in great sickness wearily
I forced myself to sit upright
And found myself all dresst in white
In woodland, in the middle night.
I marvell'd, and was ill, and drows'd.
Then, as the drug passt off, I rous'd
And knew I had been druggd and stripp'd.
I was a pigeon pluckt and clippt . . .
My money, clothes and shoes all gone.
The long white coat that I had on
Was Rector's cricket-umpire coat,
Tied by the sleeves about my throat
But for that mercy I was bare.

I staggerd out into the air
And knew not where I was, but knew

That I had fallen on a crew
Of thieves, in spite of every warning.
And what would happen in the morning
When Mother learnd the kind of ass
Her well-belovéd first-born was?

How I had been a fool and taken
The simplest bait a knave had shaken.
Fifty pound bank-notes and my pride
Lost utterly: I sat and cried.

Still dizzy with the drug I trod
Out of the woodland to a road.
There, by the moonlight and a brook
I recognized the way I took
And knelt in the cool mud and drank
Like a parcht horse and gave God thank
And drank again, and yet again
Like meadows in the May in rain.
And splasht my face, then tottered down
Bare-footed to the sleeping town
And as I went each stone beneath
Seemed full of thorn and foxes' teeth,
And I was cold and sick and sad.
O friends, I was a sorry lad.

PART II

I had no count of Time at all
But resting there on turnpike wall
Not sure of getting to the Station
To tell the police my ruination
I saw a dim light move and falter
In the Lady Chapel, near the altar.
And though the old monks' ghostly lights
Are seen there on the Feast Day Nights
I didn't think of those, nor feared.
The very thought of helpers cheered.
I thought: "O joy, the Rector's there;
Some midnight service 't is, or pray'r;
Or quire practice, where there'll be
Somebody to look after me."

At that the church-clock sounded One.

And as the echoes ceast to stun
And no strokes followed, Nine or Ten
I thought "The light is not of men
But spirits: ghosts are walking there."
I felt a pricking in my hair.

H

This Lady Chapel's builded fair
Out from the Church's end: it stands
Like something thought, not made with hands.
Why, at that hour was it lit?
I grippt the wall and lookt at it.

*   *   *

The light would now be dim, now glowing
Like candle-light when winds are blowing.
I shook to think of what thin crowds
Might there be flitting in their shrouds.
And then Clink, clink, I heard a pick
Strike stone and falling fragments click.
I said "Whoever works on stone,
It isn't ghosts, but flesh and bone."

So up I rose and crept anear.
Within the Chapel I could hear
Work of some sort, like an assault
With crowbars on a burial vault.
I crept right round it, to the door.

And all old tales, heard long before
Of body-snatchers, thrilled me through.

I trod the graves all wet with dew.
The chapel door was opened wide
And lantern candle-light inside
Wavered and made the shadows shake.

I crept. A muffled voice said "Take . . .
Catch hold your end. There. Got him? Hoist."

The sweat upon my brows was moist.
But still, I peept within to see
What all this midnight work could be.

I saw a man bent at a hole
Dragging with all his very soul,
Cursing, at something hard to drag,
A pick lay on a broken flag.
A lantern lit the scene: below
A voice said "Heave and make her go."

And at the heave a leaden roll,
Corpse-shaped, came endwise from the hole.
And as the coffin jolted forth
A Newgate face, all fringed with swarth,
Peered from the hole: a man crawled out.

He said: "We won't be long in doubt.
Cut open: where's the chisel, Jack?"

They cut and bent the cover back
They held the light to the cut gash.

Jim said: "His Lordship's not so brash
As when they put him in: but, look . . .
Gold rings and chain and golden crook
Empty him out, his noble nibs."

A jawbone and some scraps of ribs
And dust and gold and femur bones
Were emptied out upon the stones
And those two ruffians with delight
Held up the gold against the light
And pawed the dust and scraped the lead.

"That's all," said Jack. "Now let's to bed.
There's more in this night's work than beer."

The moon had risen high and clear
Though waning, when they rose to go.

What prompted me I cannot know
But as they left the door I raised
One hand, and held them as though crazed
I cried "Why are you robbing me?
Restore my corpse's property."

I, the half-naked thing in white
Half seen in moon and lantern-light
Must have seemd walking-corpse or ghost.

The robbers bleated like the lost
Then they both screamd and darted past
Screaming, and as they ran they cast
Their takings from them, right and left.

And one thing, scatterd from their theft,
Hit me: I pickt it up: a ring
Set with a ruby for a king.

Before St. Laurence' bell struck Two
I told my tale t' Inspector Drew
He called his men, and by Two-twenty
They found that Rector's house was empty . . .
Rector on holiday, my thieves
Gone, having sackt it, floor to eaves.

Maggie, the neighbour's child and Ann,
My so-called sister, and her man
All gone, that three who kept a school
For teaching wisdom to a fool.
All vanisht somewhere, not by train.
I never had my notes again.

Years afterwards, it chanc't, I saw
At trial in a court of law,
A man condemned for poisoning.
If I am sure of anything,
I'm sure the poisoner was he
Who wiled and druggd and plunderd me.
And one poor woman bent with sobbing
Was Ann who lured me to the robbing.

Victims need never rage and curse,
Life's justices will punish worse.

As for the robbers, Joe and Jack,
Who fled, they never ventured back.
They disappear'd into the Fair,
The better Christians for the scare.

The gold that they had scattered, prov'd
To be a crozier, chased and groov'd,

A ring and crucifix and chain
Of some old Abbot who had lain
Down in the vault six hundred years.
Some Abbot Hayward it appears.

My ruby ring, as treasure found,
Was valued at a thousand pound
Of which eight hundred came to me.

I bought the best team that could be,
I gave the village-school a tea.
I bought my Mother all a store
Of things I'd heard her hanker for,
Beside a watch and silken gown.
I had the orphans out of town
For cake and sports: the rest I bankt,
And so I ended, God be thankt.

EVAN ROBERTS, A.B.,
OF H.M.S. *ANDROMACHE*

THIS gallant act is told by the late Montagu Burrows, on page 67 of his *Autobiography* (Macmillan & Co., 1908, 8s. 6d.). I thank his son, Sir Montagu Burrows, K.C.I.E., for permission to make this use of it. The act was done in the night of the 29th-30th October, 1836, on and near the main topsail yard of H.M.S. *Andromache*, twenty-eight guns, then at sea in a cyclone not far from Madras.

The hero, Evan Roberts, was a merchant seaman of Liverpool, born at Temple Lane, and living, when ashore, at Rice Street, in that city. He was a single man, aged twenty-four at the time, had been nine years at sea, and had joined the *Andromache*, as a volunteer, at Capsingmoon, on 4th October, 1834. He remained in the *Andromache* as a main topman, till she paid off (probably at Spithead) on September 28th, 1837.

I cannot learn what became of him. He was "a quiet steady fellow" who "had through temperance become a religious man." He was of a ruddy complexion, with brown hair and gray eyes; he stood five feet four inches in height; he was tattooed with a cross on his left arm, a man and a woman on his right arm, and an anchor and A R on his right hand. If anyone who reads this can tell me more of him, I shall be grateful if he or she will write to me, in the care of the publishers of this volume.

About the ship *Andromache* the cyclone blew,
After heavy running they had to heave her to,
Seas broke green aboard her, men couldn't keep
    their feet,
The weather main topsail parted at the sheet.

The topsail lifted and split to seven rags
That streamd like banners and bellowd like stags;
Buntlines and cluelines snapt like lady's lace,
And snap at both the yardarms went the topsail
    brace.

They steadied on the lifts, but the lifts broke, too;
The topsail yard lifted and shook the frigate
    through;

The topsail yard lifted and the parrel gave . . .
And the yard went flying till the heartstrings
    clave.

Out it streamd to leeward like a wind-blown vane
Floggd its tatterd topsail and thunderd in again
Outboard at the rising, inboard at the 'scend
At each in crashing as though it were the end.

As the topmen struggled to bring it to a check
It struck on Robert Eadie and knockt him to the
    deck.
Fifty feet of timber with will and strength to
    strike
None of all the topmen had ever seen the like.

It was blind black midnight, blowing like the Pit,
The yard was flying with Death to whom it hit;
Roberts took a brace end, bit upon it hard,
When the yard crasht inboard he leapt upon the
    yard.

Now he was above it, now he was beneath,
He bit upon the brace-end and kept it in his teeth;
Tattered topsail flogged him, the blind yard
    bang'd

he top said "Glory . . . he is born to be
 hanged."

oberts reacht the yard-arm and grovell'd to the
 block,
he yard boxt compass like hands upon a clock.
ongues of flying topsail lickt away his skin
Ie rove his weather brace-end from outboard in.

oberts bit the brace-end, and gatherd as she
 swang,
eady for the life-spring a second ere the bang;
s the yard crasht inboard he leapt into the top
he topmen snatcht the brace-end and the yard
 came stop.

he topsail yard jolted, but the curb came taut,
hey dragged it into harness like a mad bull
 caught.
nderneath a staysail she pointed to the blow.
oberts and the topmen were piped below.

In case some find it difficult to follow what happened, it may be said that the topsail yard, a spar of wood fifty feet long, dangerous with tatterd gear, was flying about in the night in the gale, held only by the halliards. In the confusion and fury of darkness and storm those aloft could not explain to those on deck, nor these see. Not one man in ten million could have imagined that a yard so flying could be bridled by leaping onto it in the dark, dragging a rope, groping out to the yard arm as it flew, passing the rope through a block, bringing the rope's end in, and then leaping with it from the yard into the comparative stability of the top, all this in a furious gale at midnight with the ship so labouring that the masts threatened to go overboard at every roll. Not one man in a million could have been strong, quick and ready enough to do the deed; nor could the valour of the man have availed without the skill and courage of his shipmates.

THE WILD SWAN

PROLOGUE:

ONCE, long ago, a British Princess stood
Upon this hill, and waited while men rac't
Round what is Wootton, and the Ancient Wood
Past Chilswell to an end by Sunningwell.
Eight princes lasht their horses and stood brac't
On leaping cars in that mad feast of haste;
She, as the Prize, awaited what befel.

Perhaps she stood upon this very spot
Waiting the news, which of those hurtling peers
Winning the race should be her mortal lot.
One of the eight was Brutos, Prince of Troy.
Since then the world has ag'd three thousand years
Over their dust the rabbit shakes his ears
And sidelong falling peewits cry their joy.

111

WILD SWAN:

Last night, at stormy sunset, within the palace,
A fisher cried to my father, "Great King Berroc
A ship of strangers is beating for the harbour,
A green galley with a red sail blown to tatters
And drencht men whitened with the scurf of sea
     salt
Plying at oars, sea-weary, to come to shelter,
And at their mast's foot, lo, two marvellous
     horses
White, such as men have never seen for splendour.
Come, bringing ropes and horses and many
     people,
That, if she miss the harbour we still may rescue
Those strangers, those gleaming horses and that
     green ship."

Then King Berroc, my father, bade all men
     follow
Down to that beach of drowning; they hurried,
     they ran.
I, too, followed; and, lo, there, marvellous
     oarsmen

Pulling, like heroes to save their galley from
    wreck
A prince, clear-browd as a god, was captain of
    them.
White horses gleamd at the mast with gold
    starr'd brows.

Now they would draw away, then again drift
    shoreward.
I watcht their battle with death, little hope was
    there:
Then darkness fell, I could watch no more, but
    went.

At midnight, my Father, coming in wet, with
    lanterns,
Told that the tide had swept them again to
    seaward,
But that the sea grew worse, that the wind had
    increast.

All night, in mind, I have watcht that staggering
    ship
Of friendless strangers beating in vain against
    Death,

And pray'd that she might escape. What ship can
    she be,
Green, having painted eyes, bearing gold hung
    horses?
Marvellous horses; white; like immortal horses?
Who is that prince with the steady hand on the
    helm?
These western islands never before beheld such.

There is a stranger here in my Father's Council,
The Elder, Lykaon, who comes from none knows
    whence
He, seeing that ship, was rapt to passionate tears.
He has beheld such, surely, in times long past.

All night the tumult of wind has cried with voices
"A change is coming, the old is blowing away."
Spirits have ridden the darkness above the palace,
Spirits of Kings and Queens whom the land
    reveres still.
And lo, this morning, an oak-tree torn by the
    roots
Near the palace gates, has flung forth a golden
    crown.

These are omens and portents of change im-
    pending.
Indeed this summer is fraught with changes for
    me:—
My Father, having no heir, our island custom
Decrees, that I, the Princess, shall straightway
    marry
That prince who shall win the two-horse chariot
    race.

Princes will race on the Downs for me this
    summer,
Arrogant princes, like Prince Conan of Eire;
Masterful princes, like Prince Erbin; or witless
Like Howel, of this side Severn, or capable,
And yet not thoughtful nor subtle, like Math of
  Kent;
Or loutish, like Llywarch, the half-bred Prince
    of Wye;
Or snakes like Cradoc of Cornwall, the viper pale.

Yet one of these, or another, will lash swift
    horses
Into the Straight, ahead, and will win me there
As the custom bids, and I shall be his till Death.

Queen, as my Duty bids; whether happy who
    cares?
The needs of the Kingdom count, not one
    woman's want.

Moonlike and starry Spirit who guardest here
The difficult ways of women as they wed;
Save me from any of the men I fear,
The brute or fool or false that women dread.
Whatever life be in me let it spring
To help that rider fittest to be King.

And since a prayer may go up and down
The world of spirits seeking for a friend,
In all the markets of each starry town,
Until it find the helper to its end,
Grant that this find its Helper who shall strive
Urging that fittest, as the chariots drive.

And since those strangers helpless on the sea
Are like to women in unhappy Fate,
Grant that they come ashore where comforts be
That human love may stablish their estate;
And grant that thoughts of friends may make a
    peace
About this country till her story cease.

But here is Lykaon, who comes with strange
    tidings.
What is amiss, Lykaon? Has the ship foundered?

LYKAON:

She entered the port at dawn. I come from the
    King
To welcome her men ashore as the country's
    guests
Behold them already landed; strange men,
    yonder.
Princess, describe them: they may be my friends
    of old
I cannot look, for my tears: what are they, lady?

WILD SWAN:

They are men wearing scarlet cloaks, having arms
    of bronze
Gleaming with gold, and they lead white, gold
    hung horses
Their prince comes hither: I must not stay till he
    come.

                   [She goes.]

LYKAON:

God of my city, they cannot be what I think.
Unless a miracle come, or to-day be dream.
Their chieftain comes: this is never a dream but
    truth.

[BRUTOS *enters.*]

Welcome, sea-wanderer, to King Berroc's
    Kingdom.
The King bids you and your fellows heartily
    welcome.

BRUTOS:

To the King and you we render our hearty
    thanks.

LYKAON:

Stranger and guest, can it be that you come from
    Troy?

BRUTOS:

We came from Troy. It is nearly a year since then.

LYKAON:

Is Priam, the King of Troy, still alive, still King?

BRUTOS:

King Priam is dead.

LYKAON:

Is his Queen alive?

BRUTOS:

She is dead.

LYKAON:

Friend, ruin has fall'n upon that wide wayed city.
Is it not so?

BRUTOS:

Why should it be so? Who are you who speak of
    Troy?

LYKAON:

One who once loved her: I know that in happy
    days
The Sun God's seven white horses splendid with
    gold
Stood in the Sun God's stalls at the temple
    entrance

Fronting a green grass plot. I know that the
    Trojans
Treasur'd those white strong stallions sacred to
    God
As guards of the city's splendour, her Fortune's
    self.
You come here bringing two of the sacred horses
Deckt with the temple trappings, I therefore am
    sure
That the temple has been destroyed, that Troy
    has fall'n.

BRUTOS:

Troy has fall'n, her gates are burnd, her towers
    wreckt
Her men are slaughterd, her women are led away,
There is no Sun God's temple but two starvd
    horses
Nor any Troy, nor Trojan, but ten men homeless.

LYKAON:

Troy was not friendless, but Queen amid hosts
    of friends
What chanc't, that her army and allies faild her
    need?

BRUTOS:

Achilles, the swift-foot spearman, with all his men
Sackt the high towerd cities of half our allies.
The world came against Troy. Our spearmen
    were beaten.

LYKAON:

In telling of utmost grief there is sometimes
    peace.
How did it happen that terrible war thus smote?

BRUTOS:

My brother, Paris the prince, visited Sparta,
And stole the wife of the Spartan King, Queen
    Helen,
And carried her thence in a country ship to Troy.

The Spartan King, with his brother, the King of
    Argos,
Gathered a fleet, encampt at Skamander mouth
And fought with Troy for the winning back of
    his Queen.
Nine years they fought, for as fire begins in grass

And creeps, till a gust take hold, when the fire
    lifts
Till the thorns and the gorses catch and the
    crackling leaps
Into the cedars and pines till the forest flames,
So warring spread from the city to distant tribes,
Hardly a city or island or tribe of men
But sent her strength to the war, for or against us.

I know not utterly how the Argives triumpht,
Those who could tell were killed, but we heard
    long after
A trader tell this tale of the Argives' cunning:
They sent away some ships from their forted
    beaches
To make us think that their army was raising
    siege,
Then in the laxness due to our rapture at peace
Some of their pickt men enterd our city unknown
Disguisd as our outland allies and hid themselves.

Then, in the darkness, the best of their spearmen
    rankt
A few at a time, unseen, near the western wall.
It was hot dark moonless summer with river mist,

Sentries and gate guards thought that the war
    was over.
Suddenly those pickt enemies leapt and knifed
    them
And flung the Southern and Skaian gates wide
    open
And the waiting spearmen rusht and the wall was
    won.

I was asleep in the palace: I woke to cries
I thought "Some spearmen are quarrelling over
    dice."
It was dim morning with light upon Ida's top.
Then I saw sparks of fire from blazing thatches
And heard the trumpets of Argives blowing the
    charge
And cries from our men alarmd and the clash of
    bronze
Clanging on bodies falling. I cried "A surprise ...
The Argives are on us. Wake."
                      We sons of Priam,
Snatcht spears and ran to the lane where the
    trumpets blew.
My father Priam was with us; we held the lane
That led to the Skaian gate, for some of our men
Had flung some hurdles across as a barricade.

We tore down doors, draggd settles, tables and
    benches
Onto this barricade, while the light grew greater
A clanging of bronze arose at the other gates,
And arrows with blazing tow fell over the wall.

Then a great, mad moody chief with a shield that
    gleamd,
Swift Foot Achilles, he who had slaughterd
    Hektor
And draggd his corpse round Troy at the chariot
    tail,
Thrust up the lane through the Argives followed
    by three
Red-plumed hill swordsmen: "Out of my way,"
    he shouted,
"Out of my way, you Trojans, Troy is now ours."
He leapt on our barricade and over it, down
Stabbing, stabbing, stabbing, and at each stab
    mocking
Our stand was broken and Priam was stabbd,
    Troy lost.

Some of our men clos'd up round my wounded
    father.

We drew him out of the fighting into a house:
He said "The city is lost; rescue her glories,
The horses of God, the cloak on Athena's shrine,
Run to Athena's and to Apollo's temples
O save those holy things from the Argive
    clutches,
We women and men must die, the city must burn,
Those splendours, gifts of the gods themselves
    must be sav'd."
Then rallying at his death, a god spoke through
    him:
"I charge you leave me: save horses and cloak: a
    curse
On any who turns aside till those things are
    sav'd."
So saying, he shook and droopt and his hands
    unclencht.

We ran, too late, for blue-scarved Locrian
    reivers
Were already breaking Athena's temple doors.
Some of us turned to attack them, but I, with a
    few
Ran to the green grass close at Apollo's temple
To save the horses before we could be cut off.

Friend, it was no light matter to save those horses,
They were mad with the smell of blood and the
     sight of fire,
They were biting the brazen chest-bands that
     bound them in,
And kicking the bronze shod stalls; they reard,
     they hennied.
When we got them out and had mounted, where
     go then?
Troy seemd surrounded, all of her gates were
     assaild.

But suddenly swift Achilles with red-plumed
     spears
Was on us, we fled, and the fire bright bronze of
     spears
Flasht by our eyes as we fled: the bronze of our
     friends
Clangd as they fell; and we rode at the northern
     wall
Since all other ways were barred: men seeing us
     pass
Struck at us cursing, that we were deserters flying,
And the women wailed, "God's horses are
     leaving Troy."

There was no way out of Troy but the rampart's
    top.
We set the horses at that, and the horses knew,
They glared, and their hoofs struck fire, their
    nostrils snorted,
We cried as we lifted them on, they launcht, they
    leapt
Up at the parapet, over the parapet.

And the Sun God, leaping, white bright fire from
    Ida,
Bore us up at the rocks that we did not perish.
The seven landed and gleamd and their nostrils
    flamed
And the temple guards leapt after and joind us
    there,
They buried their hands in the manes of harsh
    bright hair,
Together we scrambled down the rocks to the
    plain.

But there in the plain were the chariots and the
    lancers
Of Argives watching the sack: they saw us at
    once,

A troop of their lancers turnd and the chariots
 turnd
And as we galloppt to northward, they, too,
 galloppt:
We galloppt into each other at Simois' ford
Trampling the dimpling brook with its yellow iris
Staining the shallows with blood as we fought
 for life.

They killed us Asteropæus, Ilos, Hylas,
Three of our best, and three bright horses: we
 broke them,
We rode out clear from the ford: we were fifteen
 men
Riders and temple-keepers: we rode to the north.

We knew not whither to go among Troy's allies;
Some said Apæsus, others the western mainland,
Others said back to Troy when the Argives have
 gone,
But I said "Friends, our chances of life are
 slender.
Look there to our right and front at the Argive
 horse.

Those green-scarved men are our enemies wait-
    ing us;
And behind us, look, we are followed: Lancers
    come."

And indeed those Argive raiders had shut us in.

We turnd to the Straits side, thinking there to be
    killd.
But Apollo, our city stay, had prepar'd help. . . .
There, drawn up on the beach, was a green curvd
    galley
I galloppt thither and cried, "Lo, friends, a
    marvel.
This ship has come to-day from the Scythian Sea,
With horses for Agamemnon to ride his raids.
Horses and pirates, both, are away at the sack.
Here is the ship with her horse-pens, water and
    hay.
Hurry the horses into the pens, come, hurry,
Quick, ere the Greeks are on us: we still can be
    saved,
Quick, get the horses aboard."
                        No minute was lost,
Swiftly we hurried the horses into the pens
Then we rallied the galley down on rollers

Into the sea, then leapt aboard as she floated
Ran to our oars, swift sculling and hoisted her
    sail.
There we were out in the ice-cold current driving
As Greeks came gallopping into the water
    cursing,
Hurling their darts, dismounting and hurling
    stones,
But we were away, four horses and fifteen men.

Then, with a shriek, and with cloud, the north
    wind took us
As we drove by the camps, we saw Troy blazing
    high
With tatters of flame blown streaming: blackness
    closing.
We were cityless, wifeless, childless, homeless,
    strays.
At night in that tempest driving we sometimes
    saw
Gleams in the islands, lights, or a herdsman's
    fire,
Or lantern of one going home: we had no
    home.
The green-faced god was grim at our going by.

LYKAON:

I know how grim: I have saild in those northern
    storms,
Those ice-cold blasts from the mountains,
    withering men.
Seas flying high on the islands, sails in tatters.

Friend, in my boyhood, I should have curst
    Troy's sackers
So that my hate should have gone like a living
    thing
Fastening into their lives as sickness fastens
Till they fell to ruin and died enslav'd, cast, faln.

But I hate and curse no more: I have learnt too
    well
The power of life to hurt those living on earth.
A passionate wrong cries ever till judgment
    comes.
But I interrupt your tale, Son of King Priam.

BRUTOS:

In the grayness and wildness before the morning
The horses whinnied and, lo, a brightness
    lighten'd

Ship and tackling glowed like white-hot embers
    burning
In the furnace of a potter or a sword-smith.
And the horses screamed and all the cocks of
    earth crow'd
And with clanging cries white fire-eagles lighted
Upon the yard and in unbearable blazing
The Sun God's self, the destroyer of the darkness,
Spilled his Light and Health upon us, singing
    to us,
From the space among the horses at the mast-foot.
Comfort he gave us and healing; this was his song.

    Light follows darkness, friends: advance.
    The old thing dying gives new chance.
    Venture, for to the muscles' ache.
    The net comes gleaming in with take.
    Venture: possess the river pools,
    The wallows of the shag-brow'd bulls,
    The reeds of the lagoon, the sea
    Ruled by my lesser mystery;
    But take, and make your own, the grass
    Where yet no cornfield ever was
    Where wild mares run; oh make your own
    That fiery thing of blood and bone
    The Horse, for you shall live by him:

The Blood Horse with the muscled limb,
The kindling, startling, nervous eye,
The vein-work wrinkling in the thigh,
The bright skin that the foam-flecks stain,
The tense head leaning on the rein,
The bronze shod, rounded, thundering feet
Running as wind runs over wheat,
Running with other racing hooves
To one great tidal face that moves
White, under banners at the goals:

And in the broad-loin'd mares with foals
In deep grass when the cuckoo tolls,
In these shall be your joy and wealth:
Your pride shall be the grass in health,
The plough-teams dragging the bright share,
The cart-teams dragging wains that bear
The sunburnt bread in husk from field.
Venture: the bitter bars will yield.

Man is but as a spark aswim
In deathlessness surrounding him.
When he is most himself, he dreams;
But in his passionate extremes
He touches deathlessness.

Advance.

Limitless the inheritance;
Deathless the spirit-fields men till;
Your Heaven and Earth are what you will.

So with counsel and promise the god gave
    comfort.
But, stranger, who are you that can tell of Troy,
That are friend to Troy, that lament the fate of
    Troy?

LYKAON:

I am your brother, Brutos, the son of Priam.
Hecuba was my mother: I was her first-born.
Lykaon my name was, then, when I was a prince.

BRUTOS:

Lykaon, Priam's son? But my youngest brother
Was called Lykaon, a lad whom Achilles killed.

LYKAON:

Even my name, then, given unto another.
Was I never talkt of, then, in my father's house?

BRUTOS:

Never: yet, when I was little, I heard two maids
Talking in whispers about a Prince who was lost
Hunting, in Ida, and no trace found, long ago.

LYKAON:

Thirty long years ago . . . Was no message
   given?
For wanderers whom I met in my old despair
Promist to give my father word of my woe . . .
They did not then? A promise to men in grief
Is lightly broken . . . they never knew what
   happen'd?

BRUTOS:

Not that I know. Doubtless they mourn'd you,
   my brother,
And word went round that your name should
   never be said.

LYKAON:

Did not the hunters tell of me? Was no song
   made?

BRUTOS:

You know how people respect the sorrow of
   Kings.
I, the King's son, heard neither your story nor
   name.
What is your story, brother? What changed your
   fate?

LYKAON:

I rode to the Idan glens in a day of Spring.
I rode to a gray-green wood where the stags were
tame,
A wood where hunters and charcoal burners of
Troy
Had never yet come: and there in the dusk I slept.

And painted Hunters of Heads from the Savage
Lands
Caught me and bound my hands with their
thongs of deer hide
Carried me thence to the sea with their bleeding
spoils
Of dead men's heads and horses and bronze
headed spears
And sold me there to a pirate out of the North . . .
And my pirate sailed that hour and bore me
thence.

Westward we went, up rivers, by savagest tribes,
Horse-eaters, drinkers of mares' milk, drinkers of
blood . . .
I was sold to a tribe of killers wandering west
For twenty years I was tosst upon tides of war

For twelve years past I have livd as counsellor
    here
To good King Berroc, the king of this western
    land.
I have been tosst by peoples, you by the ocean
That has less mercy than men: how came you
    hither?

BRUTOS:

By storm undying, blown westward then blown
    northward.
You see us now sea-broken, unfit for sailing
In a leaking, sinking ship without provision
Nor tackling, no, nor seamen, and no returning,
No hope of going forward, or building anew.
But come, with the Sun God's horses, here to an
    end.

LYKAON:

Brother, the Sun God brought you. King
    Berroc bids you
Welcome ashore; yourself and your men and
    horses
Knowing that the gods come among men as
    strangers.

137

BRUTOS:

Strangers are hated: hatred will be our portion.

LYKAON:

This land is gentler to strangers than to her
    own.
Besides you carry means of coming to glory:
The gleaming stallions, the horses of the Sun.
King Berroc has no son, his heir is a daughter.
It is the land's law, stablisht here from of old
That an heiress shall be rac't for upon the
    down
By unmarried princes driving in two-horse
    chariots.

Courage: Apollo brings you here for the race
So bring your horses ashore and harden them
    here
And race on the windy down for the lovely girl
And heritage here of the good King Berroc's
    crown.
Apollo has brought you: venture for fame and
    state.
Sorrows oft bless those who endure to wait.

[*They go off.*]

THE WILD SWAN

WILD SWAN: [*Discovered.*]

Ev'n now the chariots race around this hill
At fullest gallop, with myself for prize;
Those princes' panting horses agonize.
And I, O Heaven, my very heart stands still.
Each of those seven *may* win, and one will
And which, ah, which? For Destiny, who bides
Hidden above all Contest, She decides
Whether to crown a striver or to kill.

And out upon that track are Accident
Envy and Murder, and those littlest things
By which What Is To Be confuses Kings,
The Will of God confounding what man meant.
I saw those seven champions as they went
Out to the field . . . But now my hopes must be
Unuttered. Destiny decides for me
I, the Princess, abide the Fortune sent.

These are the seven Princes who compete:—
Erbin, who rules from Snowdon to the Dee;
Keen-witted as the eagle-cock is he,
And sudden in his mind as on his feet.
He drives two stallions, black as mountain peat.

His colours are a pale blue splasht with gold;
He means to be a story that is told,
Ambition is his spirit's daily meat.

Then Howel comes, from Bredon, driving grays;
Blackhaird like Erbin but without the force;
A witless man, as hearty as a horse,
His colours, green. Then Cradoc comes with
    bays.
He governs moorland where the adder plays
And sea breaks upon Cornish rock; and he
Is fatal as the adder or the sea
White are his trappings, deadly are his ways.

Then, with brown horses, comes Prince Math of
    Kent
A trusty, merry, short, thick-builded man
Who takes life as it happens, without plan,
Each minute jolly and each nerve content.
Red and blue stripes his colours. With him went
Llywarch, his friend (in yellow), from the Wye,
Driving white fetlockt chestnuts that steppd high,
The prince a boor, the horses excellent.

Then Conan, from his limestone-scatterd hills
Where rivers disappear in caves and run

THE WILD SWAN

Under the ground, unlighted by the sun
Or loiter where no fish-hook ever thrills:
He drives two roans; one kicks, the other kills.
Black are his favours and his battle flag.
Bald is he; coarse; swift-footed as a stag;
And casts his scurrilous slanders as he wills.

And Brutos drives the horses of the Sun,
The two white stallions sav'd from ruin'd Troy,
Each like a king-stag stepping to his joy
With challenging nostrils tense in question.
Their spirits and their limbs exult as one
They toss their brazen bits and fling aloof
The daisy-heads from each disdainful hoof
The scarlet that they bear Kassandra spun.

And now, beneath the hill on which I stand
Those seven teams are gallopping: I hear
Below me, there, the tumult of the cheer
At some sharp struggle for the upper hand.
There they go leaping, there the spurting sand
Flies from the wheels and hoofs, and axles crash
And fallen horses kick their cars to stash
And someone dies that should have had my
   hand.

And there the man whose chattel I shall be
Through fatal slip, perhaps, in man or horse,
Through snatching at a chance by savage force,
Or by the ironic smile of destiny,
Will come to domination over me.
Now I am mine: within this quarter hour
I may have passt to Bully Conan's power,
To Howel's jokes, or Cradoc's misery.

Though as my Father's daughter I have vowed
Ungrudgingly to take the Fortune sent
Who has not learnd too late what vowings meant
In all their implications and been cowed?
O burning Sun, who scatterest the cloud,
Shine on thy servant, Brutos, let him be
Winner of this thy Kingdom, and of me.
But ah, one comes with tidings from the crowd.

[LYKAON *enters*]

LYKAON:

All hail, Princess, King Berroc's daughter and
heiress.

WILD SWAN:

And hail to you, Lykaon, bringer of tidings.

LYKAON:

I bring no tidings. I come as a loyal friend,
With warning that tidings coming may not be
    good.

WILD SWAN:

Is your brother hurt? The race cannot yet be
    done?

LYKAON:

Unhurt, thank God, though the race is not yet
    ended,
I tell the little I know: and little is good.
I went to a point, midway in the race, to watch.
There was long, long waiting, I thought they
    would never come.

But at last the cheering sounded and round the
    bend
Came Howel, the green-clad prince, with his
    team of grays,
Galloping gallantly on with a ten lengths' lead;
Then, second, Conan, in black with his team of
    roans;
Erbin, third, so close to the roans that the axles

Almost grazed at the bend: the Yellow Coat
    fourth
With high-stepping chestnuts, little likely to
    stay;
Then Math, in the Red and Blue Stripes, driving
    his browns,
A wonderful team, those beautiful, well-loin'd
    browns,
Compact, twin, powerful horses, timed like one.
Sixth was the White Coat, Cradoc; but still no
    Brutos.

I thought "He has lam'd a horse, or has lost a
    wheel
Or been crowded into the rails at the first bend;
He is out of the race already."

                       It was not so.
Last, by a dozen lengths came my brother
    Brutos.
His horses gleaming indeed but in hopeless case,
They were left at the starting-post a neighbour
    said.

So, he being out of the race, I come to say
That Math's two beautiful browns or Conan's
    roans

Must win, must have won by this; the race is over
There are footsteps on the road: it is Brutos
    come.

[BRUTOS *enters*]

Ah Brutos, I was telling of your disaster,
How you were left at the starting-post: what
    happen'd?

BRUTOS:

The corn-fed spirited horses were unruly:
The Yellow Coat's chestnuts started them
    kicking-mad,
Full half-an-hour was wasted making a line.
Just as the flag went down mine started dancing,
And trumpeters blowing cow-horns made them
    frantic,
I thought they would never start.
                 When I made them start
The rest had rounded the curve and were out of
    sight.

LYKAON:

I saw the race at its middle point, with you
    last.

BRUTOS:

I was last long after that, then the chestnut team,
Yellow Coat's team, pulled up on the rise, dead-
        beaten,
And the Green Coat driver, Howel, who drove
        the grays,
And had made the running throughout, slowed
        down and stoppt
The rise of the hill made all of the drivers glad
To slacken the terrible pace and take a pull
I even hoped to be with them ere we finisht.

But the long rise ceast, we came to the table land
Again the gallopping hoofs went leaping from
        me
Conan leading a length, then Erbin's blacks, then
        Math,
Cradoc a little behind them: even Cradoc
A dozen good lengths ahead of myself, alas.

And behold the Sun shone out, that the forest
        gleamd
I cried, "Apollo, O Lover and Lord of Troy
Apollo, come to the help of these your horses."
And galloping there, lo, sweet, a twittering
        came.

Over my head was a flutter of tiny birds,
Linnets and scarlet finches and speckled thrushes
Gleaming, and urging forward and crying
    "Swift, Swift"
Delicate reed birds such as build among bulrush
And flag, and flowering reed in Skamander
    banks.
These, too, and the herons that watch in the
    Simois pool
And I cried "Lo, God sends help," and a loud cry
    came,
"On, on, on," and behold my brothers were
    there.

I knew them there in the air although all were
    chang'd
Into spirits so bright, so fierce, so splendid
    strong
I could hardly look; our father Priam like fire,
Hektor glowing with glory seizing the reins
And the others urging the horses *On, On, On.*
And the horses knew them and glared, their
    criniers hackled
The pæan of Troy rang out; then with sweet
    sweet song
Beautiful things rusht up to us out of the air,

Our Mother the Queen, so grave, so gentle
    sweet,
Andromache lovely as dawn, so wise, so fair,
Beautiful little Polyxena the fearless,
They shed white gleaming flowers and cried *Hope*
    conquers.
Then lo, there was sudden darkness and sudden
    redness
Over us all with our straining teams red clouds
    ran
Clouds full of harpies that screamd *On, on,* and
    darted
And struck at the teams they hated, and under
    the clouds
Glowing and splendid spirits struck back or
    warded
And the air rang loud with harps and with
    whirling wheels.

As winter wanderers lost in snow on Ida
Treading the beastless, birdless, manless, loneli-
    ness
Beating the storm, knowing nothing but rock and
    snow
Suddenly reach an Edge and behold the sun-
    light

Lighting Troy and the sea and the holy islands
And the plain all bright with cities and grazing
    kine:
So, suddenly, as we galloppt, behold, the brow
Of the hill, and below, afar the long, green
    Straight
With thousands on either side and tossing
    banners.

Then, with long leaping strides we swung to the
    valley
And gallopping down the slope, lifting and
    tossing
I came to Prince Cradoc driving his failing bays
I saw his sinister milk-white meanness glitter
As an adder glitters at striking : I saw Death
Gleam in his face, as with all his failing powers
He lasht and swung his pitiful team to wreck me.
His axle gave and his pole was snappt across
He was flung to earth, and his horses swervd and
    scream'd.
We were past and on, and suddenly lo, the
    Straight.

As a sailor running a northern tempest down
In a lifting gleam will suddenly see two islands

Beaten by roaring water and bursting sprays,
A narrow channel of safety between the two
And no time left but to steer the galley and hope;
So, into that roaring channel of tossing banners
And shouting and running men and blowing
     trumpets,
Our four swift gallopping teams went thundering
     on
A flame in the horses' hearts, a flame in our
     hearts,
Math, Erbin, Conan to beat in three short
     furlongs,
All three leading by lengths: and the Post in
     sight.
Then the horses cried Aha, and the thousands
     husht.
The blackness of watching people suddenly
     stilld
The multitude made one face, one soul, wide-
     staring.

And as, in an April day, after northern storms,
A stillness falls upon Troy, and Scamander
     stays
Her roaring of spate, the sun shines, little
     flowers

Cover mountain and plain with colours and
    perfumes,
And Earth is still with the Spring, then, out of
    the South
A sighing comes in the air from birds returning,
And the cloud of the birds returning dims the sky.
Swans of the Lakes with their necks like launch-
    ing spears
Wild duck thrusting the sky like to arrows with
    barbs,
And with crying and creaking of penns the flight
    comes
Stunning the ear with the rush and the roaring
    wings
So now, to that tense crowd, the rush of our cars
    came.

And lo, in a dozen leaps, I was racing Erbin,
Level with Erbin, up to his blacks, then past
    them.
There were two cars left ahead, Prince Math with
    his browns,
And Conan's roans, our cars went leaping and
    rocking
With clicking of straining harness, with tearing
    hoofs.

As a temple bell, in a sunburnt Asian land,
Will tinkle alone at some hot sunset hour
That ploughmen halting their plough unhook
    their oxen,
And hoers, shouldering hoes, turn shambling
    homewards,
Then another bell begins from another temple
And suddenly all the bells ring out together
Till temples rock, and the great bell in the tower
Stumbles into its clanging and drowns all other
With thunder of iron laughter or sullen order;
So now a boy's cry sounded, then shouts, then
    crying,
Then all the thousands in pack gave tongue
    together
In thunder of voices "Come, Math," "Erbin,"
    "Conan,"
"Math," "Conan," "Erbin": I sicken'd, my eyes
    blinded.
Then a louder roaring grew, and behind me
    hoofs,
Mad hoofs gallopping up, and a mad voice
    crying:
It was Erbin, making his effort; lo, his team
Alongside, creeping beyond me, and all the
    tumult

Of all his tribesmen crying, "Ho, Erbin, Erbin;
Erbin is beating them; Erbin is winning it;
    Erbin."

Then all of the roaring changed to "Conan,
    Conan,
Conan will have it still. Conan will beat the
    browns,
Come on now, Conan: he's beating the browns:
    he has it."

I cried "Now horses of Troy: up: up together
Up, and be first, or die;" and the horses answer'd
"We'll do it, O prince; if our bursting hearts
    burst not."
Our four teams leapt to the finish, mad-eyed,
    mad-souled.

I saw the flag at the Post blow slowly upward
And the King's crown gleam as he bent to watch
    the end.

Then all of the race leapt up to a glare of life,
A roar arose and heightened, arose and thunder'd:
"Math has it, Math wins, Conan, Conan will do
    it.

Erbin is gaining. Come, with a wet sheet,
    Erbin.

The Trojan is in it. It is Conan's race. Conan.

No, the browns are holding them. Come along,
    Math. Math wins.

No, look at the whites, the whites, the whites,
    the whites.

The Trojan is coming through them: he's coming
    thro' them,

He'll do it. He'll do it still. He's up. He's got it.

He's up to the browns. It's a tie. It's a tie. It's a
    tie.

No, the browns have got them. Come, Math.
    Come along, Math.

Here come the browns, Math has it now. Math
    has it.

There never was such a race: dead heat: dead
    heat.

White leads: no, brown leads: they're level."

                  Then wild life came

As a high white tottering wave that glitters and
    sings,

I lifted up to the front as the post flasht by;

We whirled for a hundred yards: we won by a
    neck.

LYKAON:

Since you have won, behold the prize of the
winner.

WILD SWAN:

Since you have won, no sorrow that darkens our
life
Will seem to be sorrow: this wonder will shine in
our hearts,
Forever, like sunlight.

LYKAON:

The trumpets are sounding
Hail to King Berroc: Hail to his prince and
princess.

EPILOGUE:

Sweet friends, this Brutos marry'd the Princess,
And when her Father dy'd received the Crown.
He govern'd well his Kingdom on the Down
Bringing his enemies to nothingness.
He gave to women and the weak, redress:
To arts, encouragement and means to grow.
To men, his subjects, happy hearts to know
The spirits that en-noble Man and bless.

And when he dy'd he was so great a King
That this most blessed England then was nam'd
Britain from him (or so it has been claim'd).
And he, being dead, was laid within a ring
Of great stones gather'd where the skylarks sing.
Then they heapt earth upon the bondless stone
Thousands of years have made the place un-
      known;
The humping rabbit goes there: sheep bells ring.
The wind blows pure
His dust has made the heather-roots secure
The wild bees bless his dwelling with their
      drone.

RICHARD WHITTINGTON

Persons:

FORTUNE	RICHARD WHITTINGTON
MISTRESS MERCER	ALICE
MESSENGER	MAPONGO

FORTUNE:

I am Fortune: I give as is fitting to each of my
    souls,
Therein, as their strength is, they follow or
    fashion their fate
Though his embers be almost extinct, if I breathe
    on the coals,
The man reddens into a glory and gleams and is
    great
When I breathe not, the glow of his state
Dies down into ash on the bars.
I pass over men with my stars.

Now here, from the red clay compounded, a lad
    from the west
The son of a lord of a manor, a fortunate child . . .
My dark stars were passing, his Fortune was
    darkened with pest
Since then, in the years he has suffer'd I have not
    once smiled.

The poisonous words that make wild,
And tears, are his portion of late
My darkness will pass, if men wait.

[*She goes.*]

RICHARD WHITTINGTON:

When I was but a babe, my Father died
In the Great Death, with half his folk beside.

My Mother married with another man
A bitter time for me then soon began.

Not being wanted in my Mother's home,
And hating him she loved, I used to roam

About the forest in that hilly land
Which the Great Death had utterly unmanned.

For I could wander all day long and find
No house with any dweller save the wind;

Chapels with red deer muzzling at the paint,
Still blue and gold, of some forgotten saint

And dogrose thrusting past the carven piers
And altars where wild dogs killd the wild steers.

And skeletons of women dead of pest
With their long hair the chaffinch wove her
    nest.

There was a little town where all were dead
The winds jangled the church bell overhead

And cats came snarling: you may judge the joy
That Dead Man's Land was to a little boy.

When I was nine years old, my mother's mate
Said "He must go, this Richard, with his hate,

Off to my sister's husband there, in Cheap,
To learn a Mercer's trade and earn his keep

No longer lurk here skulking, eyeing me
With that glum hate which I am sick to see."

So here I came to learn a Mercer's trade
This is the fourteenth year that I have stayed:

The business droops, the Mercer is now dead
His half-mad widow governs here instead.

Her hatred hinders me from chance or wage
My Mother's Husband holds my heritage

By hate from both, my Fortune is oppos'd.
Last   June,   before   the   Summer   Term   had
        clos'd,

A Shipman came here, making up his trade
"Adventure everything," my instinct said.

But luckless I, with nothing but a Cat
To stake in trade could only venture that:

Now I regret I did not venture this
Body and mind, and that which in them is.

Adventur'd that and on a reckless die
For Death or Fortune riskt this grumbling I.

I would have, too, but for the love I bear
To Mistress Alice, beautiful and fair;

Daughter of Arlingham, King Richard's Knight.
She only is my pleasure and delight.

Penniless I, unhappy, love her so
That though I hate my life, I cannot go

Away from here, lest I should never see
Her blessed sunlight shining upon me.

She comes here sometimes as a sunbeam falls
Once in a year, perhaps, on prison-walls

Then, passing, leaves the knowledge that light is.
Would I had greatly ventur'd, ending this,

Staking myself for all that I have dreamt.
Love is not love that risks not in attempt.

I should have ventur'd seaward and have
    found
Way to my heart's desire, or have drowned . . .

Not rotted here . . . The tyrant enters. Peace.
                                        [*He goes.*]

RICHARD WHITTINGTON

[*Enter* MISTRESS MERCER.]

MISTRESS MERCER:

He shall not rob this old ewe of her fleece,
Whittington shall not, though he be the son
Of that old Knight who perisht in the pest.

My Brother wed the old Knight's widow, true;
And took her manors, but he found no peace
Dogged daily by this Richard Whittington
Would he had cut the infant's neckbone through
And flung him to the hounds: it had been best.
Would he might cease.
Hate of him leaves me utterly undone.

It was my Husband's being partly mad
And love for Brother made me take the lad.
Here throughout boyhood he has learned the
    trade.
Now the ungrateful scoundrel would be paid . . .
Paid, after all the charity he has had.

I know he longs to murder me and seize
My Husband's place and work-rooms: oh, I
    know

The greed of gold possessing him like lust . . .
Why, when the Captain came, some months ago,
This Richard sent his cat abroad in trade;
Ventured his cat for profit over-seas . . .
O dog, so greedy for the golden dust,
Small profit, God be thankt, your venture made;
Ship, cat and captain must have drowned ere
  this;
None has had tidings of them since they weighed.

Would that my thought were poison in his cup,
I hate him so; for I am growing old,
My star is sinking, his is rising up
This Richard rises and my heart forebodes,

For I am in a dangerous enterprise:—
My Brother, who usurps this Richard's lands,
Plots for the post of Warden of the West
Which the King gives to Arlingham the Knight.
My Brother and myself have sworn to lies
Against this Arlingham: and now, to-night,
Our joint denouncing comes to the King's hands.
God, put belief within the royal breast,
Let him believe our charges and smite down
This Arlingham, and make my Brother warden.

163
          M

But lo, the white rose comes from the rose-
    garden,
Arlingham's daughter, Alice, London's crown,
Comes hither with her simper: come, sweet Miss,
Heaven shall change that simper into tears,
And hoist your Father's head aloft on spears,
Before to-morrow's dawn, if Heaven hear me.
This poisonous Richard loves you from afar
My hate shall drag you under, moth and star,
I am old and quaking upon Death's abyss,
Before I fall, your dying groans shall cheer me.

[ALICE *enters: She calls.*]

ALICE:

Is Mistress Mercer here? Is Richard here?
I will call Hob, the foreman, for I fear
That both are out, and I must leave a word.

[*Enter* RICHARD.]

RICHARD:

Greetings, sweet lady.

ALICE:

                Richard, you have heard
How latterly the King, in his great grace
Has honoured us in Court with pride of place.
He has made my Father Warden of the West
To hold the Marches that the Welsh infest,
And we must start at once, and shall be gone
Three years, my Father thinks, or thereupon.
I come to tell you this, and say farewell.
I know this bitter place has been a hell
To you, these latter years, and is so still.
Believe that Life will better and it will;
I, as your Friend, most fixedly believe
That you will conquer Fortune, and achieve,
And soon, an end to all your misery.
I shall think often of you: now good-bye.
If I can help in friendship in the West
In righting you where you were dispossesst
Count upon me, upon my Father, too.
But of your own strength you will struggle
      through
These bitter times and be the man I think.

RICHARD:

'Couraged by you a man will never sink.

I am happy at the honour that has come.
May you be happy in your Western home;
I shall think much of you and wish you well.
What you have been to me, no tongue can tell.
Through these last months, your sometimes
        coming here
Has been like sun in April of the year.
May all good angels be about your ways;
And if, as God forbid, unhappy days
Should ever come, that you should need a friend,
I am devoted yours till the world's end
And should be proud to aid you till I die.

ALICE:

I know it, Richard, thank you: now good-bye.
Good fortune to you in the days to be.
                    [*She goes.*]

RICHARD:

Love flows like Severn, but it ebbs like sea.
She mounts, she rides away, and she is gone . . .
Three years, her Father thinks, or thereupon . . .
How can a life continue without sun,
Without the hope of light or coming Spring?
Would men were as the swallows that can wing

After their heart's desire anywhere.
Would I had ventured with the sailors there
With my poor cat, to better Fate or end.

MISTRESS MERCER:

Believe in Life, good Richard: it will mend,
And you will conquer Fortune very soon
And be as glad as April in the moon
And follow Alice on the swallow's wing.
Why, you bone-idle, gormandizing thing,
Why, you shall have your wouldings to the top:
I here dismiss you, both from works and shop,
Go venture with the sailors like your cat,
Or after Alice as the swallows do.
The world's your mistress now: I've done with
    you.
Forth with you to the beggary and rope
Henceforth to be your portion as I hope.
                               [She goes.]

RICHARD:

Since I am cast, I will go westaway,
After my heart's beloved, and assay
Adventure for her, though I nothing have
Beyond the wits and thews that Nature gave.

Her Father may engage me in his troop
Riding the Marches beyond Severn Loop,

And I will serve him well, serving for her,
And it is good to plunge into the stir

For her who is the banner of my mind.
Therefore I go, to seek what I shall find.

[*He goes out.*]

FORTUNE:

I am that Lady Fortune whom men paint
With globe or turning wheel, forever swift,
Whom many men implore, as to a saint,
Out of the drowning waters as they drift.
My weathercock, that shows how the winds
    shift,
I bear aloft, for wandering men to see,
It swings in the bright sun on the blue lift,
And men beholding are aware of me.

About a central calm the currents turn,
Gently or turbulently, never still;
As round a rock the tidal eddies churn,
So these, as the Mood passes at my will.

And as men lift their eyes towards a hill
For marching-mark when wayless in a plain,
So, in the darkness of the roaring ill,
Men question this, "Does Fortune turn again?"

O shifting winds of passion, changing tides
Of living nations that the women bare,
Seek out the central quiet that abides,
Within yourselves are Peace and Everywhere;
But since the running star with the bright hair
Lures, and men follow, to disaster strange,
Think this, that I am just, and am aware,
And that, however fixt, the wind will change.

[She goes.]

RICHARD:

Alas! for changing Fortune; for a blow
Has laid my Alice and her Father low.

I left this city for the West, I passt
Into the springless Cotswolds, scanty-grasst,

And saw the raddled Severn running red,
With Worcester green, and Malvern blue, ahead.

Then learnd that on some traitor's false report
Alice's Father was disgrac't at Court

And had return'd to London to await
Sentence (men told me) and a traitor's fate,

With ruin to himself and to his girl.
Thus, with my wits and passions in a whirl

Helpless in Alice's need as in my own,
I sat me down upon a boundary stone

Not knowing where to turn, nor what to do.
And as well-water, ever-clean and new,

Comes from the unknown hollow underground
Into the light, and dances, and makes sound,

So, from within me and without me, wells
Of message sounded with the voice of bells,

Saying again and yet again, these words.
    "Turn again, Whittington,
    Lord Mayor of London Town;

Turn again, Whittington,
Lord Mayor of London Town;
Of London Town
Three times Lord Mayor."
The April wind and all the April birds

Repeated this, so that I could not doubt
My Life within was toucht by Life without.

Therefore I have returned as the words bade.
I hear sad news of my beloved maid.

Her Father's goods escheated to the Crown,
Herself in some mean lodging in the town,

Deserted in her need, and helpless I
Her friend forever, sunk in poverty,

But I am in the cockcrow of my day
After the dark, the morning becomes gray.
Beauty will triumph, Love will find a way.

                              [*He goes out.*]

[ALICE *enters.*]

RICHARD WHITTINGTON

ALICE:

Since we are ruin'd, since my Father's fine
Is far too heavy ever to be paid
I have forgotten that the sun can shine
And thought the story of my fortunes said.

Father, unjustly 'prison'd in the Tower,
Lives with small hope of ever issuing thence
He tells the dreary stones and counts the hour
And prays that God may show his innocence.

While I, deserted by the world, am now
Come to this Mercer's, seeking work to do
I have never workt, good angels show me how.

MISTRESS MERCER:

Who's there without? O Mistress Alice, you?

ALICE:

I, Mistress Mercer. May I speak a word?
I am in sorrow, as you may have heard.
And come to ask, if you can give me work?

MISTRESS MERCER:

Lace-work, or broiderer's work, or needlework?

RICHARD WHITTINGTON

ALICE:

I will learn any honest work you give.

MISTRESS MERCER:

For your amusement?

ALICE:

No, as means to live.

MISTRESS MERCER:

To live, God spare us, you are rich and proud.

ALICE:

The sun once shone: now heaven is in cloud.

MISTRESS MERCER:

Where is your Father?

ALICE:

In the Tower.

MISTRESS MERCER:

In jail?
Ah yes, for Treason; true, I heard the tale.

173

ALICE:

No, never Treason: men have falsely sworn.

MISTRESS MERCER:

Where are your friends, then: you are nobly born

ALICE:

Some are beyond the sea; some disbelieve.

MISTRESS MERCER:

They may have grounds for doubting, by your
leave.

ALICE:

No grounds, but jealousy and envious hate.

MISTRESS MERCER:

So you want work?

ALICE:

I do, I supplicate.

MISTRESS MERCER:

What sort of wages would you reckon fair?

RICHARD WHITTINGTON

ALICE:

Those paid in open market everywhere.

MISTRESS MERCER:

And bed and board besides, and holidays?

ALICE:

Whatever usual wage the Mercer pays.

MISTRESS MERCER:

I've got no work for idlers such as you.
Work is for workers, not a useless crew
Who never did a turn and never can.
You are less use than a blind, crippled man.
You that have had your riches should have
    kept.
You have liv'd daintily and ate and slept
And now will taste the difference. And besides
Treason is as the gracious King decides . . .
I'll have no traitors here, nor traitors' kin.
Find other means to feed your pretty skin,
You'll get none here and so I tell you plain.

[*She goes.*]

ALICE:

Can any offer everything in vain?
Now I perceive in what a tottering cage
Man thinks he stands above the whirlpool's rage

RICHARD:

Courage, sweet lady, for the darkest hour
Prepares the dawn, the darkest bud the flower.

Though all malignance all its malice spend
Spirits that hate malignance come to friend.

And I can friend, for everything I have
Is consecrated yours unto the grave,

Sweet lady, while I live, you shall not starve.
This city's granite block this soul shall carve

Into a setting for you, worthy you.

[*Enter* MISTRESS MERCER.]

RICHARD WHITTINGTON

MISTRESS MERCER:

Away from here, you outcast beggar's crew.
You cast apprentice with his callat, hence
Away Miss Dolly and Sir Insolence.
Off, from my doorstep, to your tavern den,
To rags of women and the wrecks of men,
To gutter-pick by moonlight for your bread,
This is no lazar house nor loitering shed
For beggars such as you to stretch and shake you.
Hence, or I'll call the watchmen who will make
    you.
And do you dare to brave me to my face?

[*Enter* MESSENGER.]

THE MESSENGER:

Is Mistress Mercer keeper of this place?

MISTRESS MERCER:

Yes, I am she, a widow, but still able
To keep a roof, and bread upon the table
For all a pack that plot to beggar me.

MESSENGER:

One Whittington was with you. Where is he?

177

MISTRESS MERCER:

He *was* with me: not now.

RICHARD:

But I am here.

MESSENGER:

In the King's name, I greet you, with good cheer.

RICHARD:

I bow to the King's grace,

MESSENGER:

God save the King,
I bear a knot for your unravelling.
So you are Richard Whittington?

RICHARD:

I am.

MESSENGER:

You recollect the queenly ship that swam
Within the Pool last year, the *London Ark*?

RICHARD:

Yes, and her Captain. Have they prosper'd?

MESSENGER:

Mark!

My tale is about them: they are no more
Their bones are in the ocean far from shore
Green water washes them and fishes eat.

MISTRESS MERCER:

Yes, and your cat's become the herring's meat,
Your cat that you adventured in your greed.

MESSENGER:

Madam, you interrupt me: pray give heed.
Although the Captain and the ship are gone
It was in battle with the Moors: anon
The mate and sailors flung themselves aboard
The Moorish ship and took her by the sword
And, ere their own ship sank, install'd them there,
Saving your cat, that pride with glossy hair.

RICHARD:

I am glad I did not send the cat to death.

MESSENGER:

You sent her to more life, for she gave breath
Soon after this to seven little ones.
She kittened, to be plain, between the guns,
And reared her kittens to a stalwart seven
Such as the cats (if there be mice) in Heaven.

The ship went loitering onward, moon by moon,
And reacht the capital of Settaroon,
Mapongo City on Mapong' Lagoon.

But, ah, Mapongo City, once so glad
With roaring life, was desolate and sad
Curse had undone the glory it had had.

Of all the roaring life that used to run
To cheer incoming bark or galleon
With songs and splashing spray, we saw not one.

Voiceless, with empty streets, the city lay,
The palm-thatch blown to tatters, witherd gray
Doors blowing to and fro, walls in decay.

And when the sailors landed, they espied

No man at all, but yet on every side
Myriads of Mice, quick-flitting, glitter-eyed.

And in the palace on his throne of state
The King of Settaroon, Mapongo, sate
Gray with his fear, but constant under Fate.

But King Mapongo comes himself to tell
How Settaroon was smitten with such hell
And how his people fled and what befell.

[MAPONGO *enters.*]

MAPONGO:

I am Mapongo. Ere my father died,
Two years ago, he called me to his side.

He said, "I tell you what my Father told
Myself, when I was young and he was old . . .

All Evil that afflicts this land of ours
Comes from a wizard who has Devil's powers.

He dwells within a man-bone scattered tract
A moon's march hence, beneath the Cataract.

He who shall kill this Devil will deliver
This Kingdom from all Evil whatsoever.

As Battle, Revolution, Murrain, Blight,
The Pest by day, man-killing Beasts by night.

Therefore I bid you (as my Father me)
Seek out this Devil (as did I and he),

And spear him if you can, ourselves have failed."

My Father having died, myself was hailed

King, in his place, and therefore took a spear
And sought that Devil in his cave of fear.

He dwells within a gash of mile-high walls
Into which wrench of earth a river falls

So that a smoke of water rises gray
All rainbow-lit and soaking earth with spray
The water-eagles cruise there, seeking prey.

I found a trackway narrow as a girth
Leading below into that gash in earth

Beneath, the water roared in the abyss
I heard the eagles mew, the serpents hiss.

I reacht the beach below, the slippery stones
Were heapt with driftwood and with dead men's
     bones.

I reacht the falls, that ever-dropping cloak
Of water torn as wool and flung as smoke.

I reacht the cave, that grimness ever gray
With ever-changing spectres of the spray.

I entered in those galleries of stone:—
I heard no sound, but I was not alone.

The black glass alleys gleam'd: I could not see
Aught else, but something else was there with me.

Its breath was just behind me as I crept,
Its footstep was like echo when I stept

At every corner, it was there in front,
My spirit was the quarry of its hunt.

And when I reacht the central cave I knew
The thing was present, evil as doom due.

And nothing shewed: a small red fire burn'd:
Yet the whole cavern threatened me and girn'd.

I cried: "I am Mapongo: meet me here
O Cavern Devil, spear to flying spear."

No answer came, yet something seemed to mock
With silent laughter in the cavern rock.

Then suddenly I felt the cavern fill
With many unseen shapes of evil will.

And suddenly a myriad little eyes
Peer'd at me from the cavern's galleries.

No word was said, but at a secret sign
A myriad teeth went 'chatter': so did mine.

Then at a sign that none could hear or see
Those myriad little Devils rusht at me.
And I? I fled, and from that hellish place
I ran to Settaroon, with them in chase . . .

And though we slaughtered myriads, myriads
    more
Came in upon us all and overbore.

We had to fly for life, and having flown
They pickt our city to the inner bone,
Nothing was left that was not shut in stone.

Hiding in forest boughs we saw beneath
The million tails, bead-eyes, and gnawing teeth,

The Mice had dispossesst us of our all.
Woe for Mapongo's melancholy fall.

THE MESSENGER:

But vengeance followed on those conquering
    Mice . . .
This Richard's cat and kittens, brought ashore,
Smote them, as blowing fire shatters ice . . .
And as November beech-leaves fly before
A gale from the Atlantic, so did these
Fly, from the terror talonning them dead.

Some, to swift ending in the breaking seas,
The rest, to darkness in the forest, fled.

The cat and kittens finisht every mouse
Down from the trees came warriors and their
    wives
Children again met parent, mate met spouse.
And thanks were sent to him who saved their
    lives.

MAPONGO:

Our friend will read the list of what we send
To Richard Whittington, Mapongo's Friend.

THE MESSENGER:

To Richard Whittington, to have and hold.
One ton of gold-dust, one ton *solid* gold.

Ten emeralds of Sarras, each as green
As hawthorn leaves in April, when first seen.
Ten rubies of Ratanga, each as red
As dog-rose berries when the rose is dead.
Ten sapphires of Solyma, each as blue
As heaven is to girls when love is new.
Ten alabaster caskets of cut stones

Amethysts, beryls, jacynths, chalcedones.
Ten sherris sapphires color'd like cut corn;
Ten moon spikes of the icy unicorn;
Ten pearls like moonlight on a quiet pond;
Ten black pearls, and a frosty diamond.

Eleven hundred ostrich plumes which foam
Over at edge in flounce as billows comb.
Eleven hundred tusks, some white and some
Yellow, some scarlet from blood-colord gum.
Eleven hundred baskets of a bark
So sweet men cannot handle it till dark.
Eleven hundred boxes of such balm
As mollifies all anger into calm.
Eleven hundred buckets of such spice
As burns the Phœnix in her sacrifice.

But topping all together comes beside
The Crimson Settaroon, Mapongo's Pride,
The jewel that gives light from inner fire,
Round as the orb, outflowing as desire,
Out of the passion of whose globe there burns
Ray after ray that lightens and returns.

Itself alone such wealth as never yet
Came Europe-wards for crown or coronet.

In all, such treasure as has never come
In any ship to any port of home.

MAPONGO:

Here is the deed of gift, the treasure waits
At Tower Wharf beside the Tower gates.
For Richard Whittington, Mapongo's Friend.
May your delight in living never end.

[MAPONGO *goes*.]

THE MESSENGER [*to* ALICE]:

Another thing, King Richard bids me say
He learns your Father never did betray,
Never, as Mistress Mercer's brother swore.
Your Father is as free as heretofore,
And has the King's great favour as of old.
But Mistress Mercer's brother is in hold
For falsely swearing, and as does appear
Usurping the estates of Richard here.
And, Mistress Mercer, I am charged to bring
Yourself to trial now before the King,
Lest you were with your brother in the plot.
Endure such fate as Fortune shall allot.

[*To* RICHARD.]

The King will greet you here when we are gone.
Long life and luck to Richard Whittington.

[He goes with MISTRESS M.]

RICHARD:

I am glad that your Father is saved from the
hatred of men.

ALICE:

I am thankful to you for your gladness and glad
of your luck.

RICHARD:

I am stunned by my fortune, your gladness alone
makes it real.

ALICE:

It is stablisht four square at the Pier like the
Tower itself.

RICHARD:

It is fortune past telling; I long for yet greater in
dream.

189

ALICE:

All the world is a ball at the feet of the fortunate
man.

RICHARD:

Sweet lady, my fortune and world are yourself
standing there,
Without you, my fortune is nothing, my world is
despair,
I love you so dearly, I cannot find words for my
love.

ALICE:

I love you so dearly, I need not the words, but
the love.

RICHARD:

O lovely belov'd, you are beauty and hope and all
peace;

ALICE:

You are gladness and comfort without whom all
comfort would cease.

RICHARD WHITTINGTON

RICHARD:

You are joy beyond telling and glory that thrills
like the sun,

ALICE:

You are desolate days put away and a new life
begun.

RICHARD:

You are all my endeavour and longing made real,
made mine.

ALICE:

Having all, each in each, let us offer up gifts as a
sign.

RICHARD:

Let us build for the wretched in prison a shelter
and home.

ALICE:

Let us build a fair study of books where poor
scholars can come.

RICHARD:

Let us dower an almshouse where bedesmen may
pass happy age.

ALICE:

Let us dower a spittal with doctors to heal and
assuage.

RICHARD:

Let us build, to Saints Spirit and Mary, a church
white and fair.

ALICE:

Let us give it a College of Priests to sing services
there.

RICHARD:

Let them sing night and day, that the Angels of
Beauty may hear.

ALICE:

And the Angels of Beauty spread feathers of gold
and draw near.

RICHARD:

And shine in this City and take each a soul to his
  fold.

ALICE:

And the souls of this City shine bright with their
  Helpers of gold.

RICHARD:

May spirits so brightened imagine the Earth that
  may be.

ALICE:

May hands so encouraged create what the vision
  can see.

BOTH TOGETHER:

May Earth be so happy with Heaven that all
  souls shall sing
          As the stars and the planets above
          The Order, the Beauty, the Love
      Of the Might that directs them as King.

THE HOUR STRIKES

PERSONS

THE SEEKER
DESTINY
KATHARINE
WOLSEY
ANNE
HENRY

THE SEEKER

The shepherds warn'd me not to climb this hill
To-night, Midsummer Night, "Because," they
    said,
"The Past goes by, with power to do ill.
And all the Kings, with Arthur at their head,
Return to life and are no longer dumb
But commune of Times past and things to come."

Yet I have climb'd the hill in hope to see,
Before the mist is white with the moon's power,
Those workers of our country's destiny,

194

And hear them talk for their allotted hour:—
And lo, great figures sitting with a Queen,
Spirits of that which will be or has been:—

O, if a mortal's question may find grace,
What are you, Lady of the starry face?

DESTINY:

Nothing, perhaps, save urging to the race.

SEEKER:

Who are the veil'd attendants at your side?

DESTINY:

Forces that spirits struck, that have not died.

SEEKER:

May I ask on, or do your laws forbid?

DESTINY:

To those who ask aright nothing is hid.

SEEKER:

Then I would ask if these are Queens and Kings
Come from this windy downland's burial rings,
Or from old tombs, on this most sacred night
To see again the land of their delight?
If so, I'll kneel.

DESTINY:

Nay, ask themselves to speak,
They were once strengths for sifting out the weak,
And resolute for ends, as you are now.
To Life's uncoulter'd pasture they were plough;
To Life's unscatter'd fallow they were seed.
They lived and suffer'd torture and had need.

And I, I dealt with them; for I am one
That trumpet up the sleepers with the sun,
And urge them on all day and blow the call
For the red sunset at the evenfall,
And new souls for the morrow. I am she
Who urges from the depths the things to be:
And millions come at call, and from their pain
Are sweated out the radiants that remain
Before I fling them by: what they achieve
I cannot count: I cannot joy nor grieve,
Only sweep on: and yet I inly know

That what they do will be my overthrow.
They will be conquerors, and I, destroy'd,
Flung forth with past abortions to the void.

But question: for at summer's topmost peak
All powers in my domination speak:
And these will speak, if question'd: but for
        me
I question nothing: only bring to be.

THE SEEKER:

Spirits, unveil to me.

[THEY *unveil.*]

                        You have the mien,
Figure and bearing of an English Queen.
O speak to me out of the night of Death.
Who were you, when your beauty drew sweet
        breath
Here on this Downland? May a mortal know?
Ha; she awakes: her life comes pulsing slow:—
She is about to answer me: she speaks.

197

K. OF ARAGON:

I am that Katharine brought out of Spain to be
 wed
To Arthur, the Prince; I was wedded, then
 widow'd, then wooed
By Henry the brother of Arthur, my prince who
 was dead:
I came to be Queen beside Henry, and sorrows
 ensued
 Not singly but brood upon brood,
 Till my heart was made sick, and my faith
 Like a rag under feet of the rude,
 And I died of the shame and the scathe.

It is scant happiness, sisters, to be as a pawn
In the chess of the Kings of the nations, a pawn
 to be play'd,
Exchang'd for advantage, or lost, or advanc't or
 withdrawn,
But the game is the game of God's will, and His
 will be obey'd.
 Like Him are the Kings He has made
 To rule as He rules, and to bring
 Into Earth the Idea of the King:
 Knowing this I endur'd unafraid.

THE HOUR STRIKES

I was a child when I was wedded to Arthur,
A child when Arthur died: yet, being a child
I saw the old King plotting to save my dowry
By marrying me to his surviving son,
Henry the Prince: he had his will and the dowry
And I was married to that most hopeful prince.

The old King died, my Henry was crown'd as
    the King.
I was the Queen of England, with bright hopes
    shining.
No prince in Europe had royaller hopes than
    mine.

How shall I speak of him that was
Of all Kings' sons the chrysopras?
He was built stalwart as the bull,
His countenance was beautiful,
His body perfect, his feet swift,
His mind fill'd full with every gift,
With every talent, for he knew
The things that men of genius do
And did them as a master might.
Music was ever his delight,
He sang, he play'd, he wrote sweet airs

Which the Court minstrels wisht were theirs:
He was an architect whose schemes
Surpasst the living master's dreams:
He knew the known tongues and could
    speak
Latin, French, German, Spanish, Greek;
And in his speech such sweetness hung
He witcht all comers with his tongue:
He knew all law, he could debate
All questions touching his estate:
In all disputes he could take part
With the best doctors in each art:
And in himself he had such force,
Such mastery and grace of horse,
Such swiftness and such skill in play,
Wrestling or tennis, that men say
None ever equalled him, or near.

In courtesy, none was his peer.
In gifts, none matcht him, nor in grace
Of body, spirit, parts or face.
None was more lov'd, none was more serv'd
With constancy that never swerv'd;
And none began a reign so stor'd
With things that men and angels hoard.

His treasuries were filled; his land
Was well content beneath his hand;
His counsellors were good; his friends
Secure; he sought no wicked ends.
The sun seem'd rising in his might
To fill the English realm with light;
And hourly the thinkers wrought
More beauty out of subtle thought.
And life, to all alive, was even
With the bright boundaries of Heaven,
And angels walkt the earth with men.
England was surely Heaven then.

And had my sons surviv'd, my Fate
Would have been ever fortunate . . .
My sons all died, I brought no heir
For all the little babes I bare.

And other bitternesses grew,
France and her influences drew
The English out of touch with Spain;
And Wolsey smarting with the pain
Of being thwarted in his hope,
Of coming to be made the Pope,
Was hostile both to Spain and me.

And Henry glower'd lustfully
On courtesans: and everywhere
Spoke of his longing for an heir
Who should ensure the Kingdom's peace.

And trouble-makers did not cease
To tell him that my barrenness
Came from his godless wickedness
In marrying his brother's wife.

Henry was coming into life,
Not reverencing aught that stood
Between him and a fancied good.
His want was master of his will.
When he determin'd on an ill,
All bent to that . . .

         So he resolv'd
To have his link with me dissolv'd,
By Papal means, if that might be.
Long, long, he wrought for that decree
By threat and bribe and argument . . .
All pretexts cloaking his intent
To leave me and to live with Anne.
I pleaded when the suit began,
Not afterward, I stood aside.

I pitied those who in their pride
Helpt Henry, then, for I had learn'd
What devil in his spirit burn'd,
What worship of himself, what will
In all things to be master still;
To be the axle or the pin
On which another world might spin.
I knew how deadly he would be
To all who helpt in ousting me;
And as I knew it would, it fell:
Their moment's glory led to hell.

I was what I had ever been,
A queen, the daughter of a queen,
Anointed and appointed great;
Death only could annul my state;
But Death came slowly: I could see
My ousters ruin'd before me.

That was no joy; I also saw
My Henry falling from all law
Into all headlong lust of will.
I saw him lie and rob and kill,
Smite at the holy, wreck the brave,
Do all things as his devil drave,

With no good counsellor or friend.
It made my very heart-strings rend
To see his soul in devil's hands.

God, who allow'd it, understands.
And, for myself, I took the bad
That followed on the good I had had.
I learn'd how pitifully kind
Friends may be to a tortur'd mind.
I learn'd that peace may be attain'd
By sinners rackt and many-pain'd;
Peace that is south wind after east,
Quiet to greatest and to least,
Quiet in which Earth's feverish things,
The wills and fiercenesses of Kings,
Sink to proportion, and the soul
Perceives the universe unroll
Star beyond singing star, immense
Beyond all dream, beyond all sense,
All order, all magnificence.

God in His Mercy let me see
Through darknesses that cover'd me
Bright planets that his angels be.

[She sinks back to her chair.]

204

THE HOUR STRIKES

THE SEEKER:

Ah, noble lady, and through you we still
Behold that light in darkness . . .

[WOLSEY *rises.*]

                                        but he speaks
To whom peers spoke bareheaded: it is Wolsey.

THOMAS WOLSEY:

I am that Wolsey the Cardinal, prelate and proud,
I who was King of my King, who was sceptre
    and sway.
To me, not to Henry, the princes and potentates
    bow'd.
I strode like the sun in his glory on Midsummer
    Day.
  My splendour all crasht in decay,
  The web that my spirit had spun
  Was swept into dust and undone;
  I died as the gambler who fails.

I was a butcher's son, but royally dower'd
With wit and Fortune, which dower smooth'd
    my pathway.

Men gave me place: men made me a priest: and
    helpt me.

One man there was who checkt me, I then being
    priest,
One Paulet, a country gentle, set me in stocks.
It is dangerous to check beginning Fortune:—
Lads grow; priests become bishops, princes take
    Kingdoms;
And I, that priest in the stocks, was soon most
    trusted,
Chaplain to Calais' treasurer, employ'd, besought,
My advice askt and taken, and my young wisdom
Praised to the King himself, who took me to
    service.
I think that Paulet repented before he died.

Henry the Seventh gave me my chance, as follows:
He sent me upon a mission to Maximilian,
The Emperor, then in Flanders: I stak't my all
On doing that mission like an angel of God.

Therefore, on leaving the King, I sped down
    river,

Helped by the wind and the ebbing tide to
    Gravesend,
Where taking horse I galloppt: and all night
    galloppt
From post to post across Kent, rousing the
    ostlers,
Flinging myself from reeking horse to the fresh
    one
And galloping through the night with owls and
    foxes,
Till lo, cocks crowed and Heaven grew gray at
    Dover . . .
There, tottering down the beach, I found fair
    fortune,
A ship with her sails cast loose at point of sailing
For Calais. I climbed aboard her; in three hours
    more
I was in France upon horseback galloping on.

That night I was with the Emperor, in treaty
None ever beat or out-brav'd me in any treaty
When I was facing my man, nor did the Emperor.
Next day my treaties were settled: all that next
    night
I galloppt for Calais, got there at morning gun

Again, found ship; and, getting aboard, wind
    favour'd,
In three hours more I was gallopping from
    Dover,
And late that night I came to the Court at
    Richmond.

King Henry being abed, I too could take rest
After eighty hours spurring from post to post,
But I was afoot ere dawn, awaiting Henry
As he passt from bed to chapel to early Mass.

He, seeing me, chid my not having started forth.
I said, "I have been: I have now return'd, O
    King."
He seem'd both startled and not well pleas'd, for
    he said:
"That is the worse, for, after you hurried away
I thought of a needful point that I had not urged
In your commission: nay, a point that was vital,
And sent one after you straight to stop and warn
    you.
Did he overtake you?"
           I answer'd, "No, Your Grace.
As I return'd I met him and learn'd his errand.

But as for the needful point, may it please Your
    Grace,
I thought of it myself on my journey Eastwards,
How vital it was; and greatly presuming dared
(Though without warrant from you) to urge the
    matter.
The Emperor's self was pleas'd to agree and seal.
Pardon your servant's assumption in so doing."

Then the King said, "I not only pardon, but thank
A servant so thoughtful, eager and fortunate."

Friends, from that mission's happy speed
Came Fortune glorious indeed.
The old King honour'd me: his son
Heapt honours on my head: I won
Glory and gratitude from men:
I was made thrice a Bishop, then
Lord Chancellor, Archbishop . . . more,
Legate and Cardinal; priests bore
Great silver crosses as a show
Before me: riches fell like snow
About me: and the gay young King
Left me to govern everything.
My will was Law in Church and State,

Through Christendom my will was great.
I said and Europe did: one hope,
One only, fail'd me, to be Pope.
The Emperor Charles betray'd me there.

I was like sunlight making fair
All that I shone upon: my house
Was beyond telling glorious
With quaintly twisted chimneys red
Above the dormers and the lead,
And halls and galleries made good
With joinery in precious wood
And flutings running down the grain.
I had stories leaded pane by pane
Into the windows, that they shew'd
Shagg'd Centaurs in the mountain-road
Coming towards the haunts of men
To ravish women: and agen
The Rapes and Loves that Ovid told.
And hanging upon rods of gold
I had tapestries of silk whereon
The Loves of Mars and Venus shone.
I had golden cups and plates enough
To fit the King with household stuff;
Of silver plate I took no heed.

My gardens sprang from foreign seed.
All that is excellent in fruit,
Or beautiful in flower, took root
There, with such fragrance, and so bright,
Spirits were trancéd with delight . . .
And I had many a joy beside:
Green woodlands for my stags of pride;
Cock-shutes and coney-warrens, stews
For many a swift pike and slow luce . . .
Half a shire grew meat and bread
That my great household might be fed.

They who beheld my state, I wis,
They only, know what glory is.
My state was greater than the King's.
My Herald went with trumpettings
Before, with the two crosses, then
My mace-man and my pillar-men,
Then ushers crying "Way, make way!"
Then three and three my pickt array
In velvet, bearing golden chains.
Then sumpter mules and baggage trains.
Then spearmen in a bodyguard
In scarlet tunics golden starred,
And bowmen wearing tawny coats.
Then to the cheering of all throats

Came the Great Seal majestical,
And the Red Hat of the Cardinal,
Both borne by noblemen; and then
I, the great crimson King of men,
Rode stately on a mule of state;
Four men with pollaxes of plate
Were at my sides, and after me
Were seventy horsemen, three and three,
Riding great horses, scarlet hung.
And men and children sweet of tongue
Sang to me as I rode or stayed.

I was a god to whom men prayed,
A wise god, taking thought for all.
In scarlet, under golden pall,
I sat like godhead and gave doom.

There were five hundred men to whom
My daily state gave daily bread.

But Henry's lust to be unwed
From Katharine and wed to Anne
Was ruin to me: there began
Problems I could not shelve nor solve.

I strove to change the King's resolve . . .
That failed . . . then I was forc't to strive
To win him licence to re-wive . . .

Yet the Pope saw what wars would be
If he should grant the King's decree.
Straight Katharine's nephew would invade
Rome, to avenge her: so he stayed.
I saw that if the Pope refus'd
The King's divorce, there would be loos't
On Rome in England, on the Church,
Utter destruction that would search
Rome's hold on England and outroot.

Such was the seed, such was the fruit.
Ev'n as I saw it came to pass . . .
That heart of flint and brow of brass
Broke Rome in England for his lust.
Myself was stricken to the dust;
That black-eyed mistress and her lord
Put some few martyrs to the sword,
And smote me to the broken form
Wrappt up in linen for the worm,
A dead man without power to stir.
I, Cardinal and Minister,

I, Chancellor and Legate, lay
Under the quire in the clay,
Dropping to dust, and all my schemes
Dust too, forgotten as men's dreams.
Forgotten as the star that lights
A trail thro' Heaven on winter-nights
And falling fades and leaves no trace.

I, the Pope's Legate, the King's Grace,
Am vanisht: there remain behind
Some gleams, however, from my mind
From which men know that there was one
Once, who was splendid as the sun;
Who bent great brows upon affairs
And made Kings' wills his ploughing-shares,
And was the central pin whereon
Revolv'd that Europe that is gone.

While I was Sun, the planets shone.

[WOLSEY *sinks back.* ANNE *rises.*]

THE SEEKER:

As you supplanted Katharine, another
Supplanted you: this beautiful blithe figure.

ANNE:

I am the beautiful Queen who was ruin'd and lost.
I am Anne Bullen, whom men still remember
    with pity.
Few have bought terrible days at more pitiful
    cost.
Falling from Queen to the hatred of country and
    city,
Like a rudderless ship I was tosst.
Powers made use of my being,
Changes too vast for man's seeing,
The Will of the Time passing by.

I was a black-eyed witty girl of old
When, with my sixteen summers hardly told,
I came from France into the English Court.

Promptly King Henry wooed me for his sport,
As he had wooed my sister (so men said);
But I escaped the amorous traps he laid.
I was the Queen's maid, dedicate and vowed
To the Queen's service, and besides was proud.

And yet it thrill'd me, knowing that the King
Lov'd me past doubt, beyond imagining . . .

That that grim palace-bull with bloody horn
Came like a ring-dove to my hand for corn.

Then, for the Queen, men mutter'd everywhere:
"A barren Queen, and England needs an heir . . .

God has pronounc't against her: it is plain.
Henry should be divorct and wed again,

The State demands it . . . If his second choice
Were English, surely England would rejoice."

Dignities fell into my father's hand,
Jewels and moneys, titles, manor-land . . .

And people whisper'd: "Lady, if you choose,
You can be Queen of England: why refuse?"

And others said: "If you were England's Queen
The Reform'd Faith would prosper and be green

Where now its martyrs perish at the stake.
Anne, become Queen for sweet religion's sake."

Others (and my ambitions) said their say:
"How grand to hear the heralds clear the way . . .

'Way for Queen Anne!'; how exquisite to lead
All England's peeresses as Queen indeed;

Call lilied France my brother, ay and bear
A future King of England, Henry's heir . . ."

When Henry sought divorce and Rome refus'd,
Bitterer tongues spoke, angrier pleas were us'd:—

"Make the King paramount within his realm,
Strike off this Roman guidance from the helm,

Abase this Spanish Queen who uses Rome.
The English King must be supreme at home."

Those whom I knew spoke thus.
                          And hour by hour
My spirit saw the images of power,

The crown, the scarlet and the pride of place,
The thousand eyes on one unseeing face,

My Father, Mother, Brother, Sister, all
Splendid with gold-work, bearing up my pall.

King Henry's hand on mine, King Henry's son
Mine, to be King when Henry's reign was done,

Were not these glories to a girl, beside
Having the great King wooing her for bride?

'Tis but a step to Hell; but getting back
Takes many a march up jagged rocks, alack!

I, who had only youth and Henry's greed,
Staked those for Henry and was queen indeed.

Rome was defied, dishonour'd, dispossest,
A flooding spring, with me upon its crest,

Swept over England, bearing me to power;
Men rang the bells for me in that my hour . . .

All England's bells . . . and London's thousands
        masst,
Scattering roses on me as I passt
To have the crown upon my brows at last.

Then great guns thunder'd, trumpets silver-keen
Shrill'd, and the Prelate cried "God save the
    Queen!"

I was the Queen, and all the battle won
If but my little child might be a son.

My child was a Princess, thereafter came
Griefs and disasters putting me to shame . . .

Daily the foothold underneath me fail'd,
King Henry weary'd of me; foes assail'd.

Men shouted insults at me in the street,
The Court spies sought my blood on catlike feet.

When foreign Kings' ambassadors appear'd
They did not hail me Queen, they smil'd and
    sneer'd

And call'd me the King's woman: but, alas,
I was not that . . . another woman was.

Jane Seymour, once my waiting-woman, stept
Into the heart that I no longer kept.

Henry and she were lovers to the full;
I was not merciful nor dutiful;

The broken heart is often mad in head.
Then was my princely little son born dead,

And I was lost.   .

                    The King deserted me;
Round me were enemy on enemy;

Some I had humbled or had thwarted, some
The friends and followers of the Queen to come.

Then I was paid that I had once revil'd
And us'd with spite my predecessor's child;

Then I was paid that once I mov'd the King
In wanton hatred to a darker thing.

I was well paid in those few weeks of hate,
Lost beyond hope, but having still to wait.

None but the lovely stand by misery.
My brother and some others stood by me.

One loyal and a lover to one lost,
Such surely is the soul God treasures most.

Bitter and utter was the death that fell
On those who comforted my weeks of hell.

In those few weeks, though nothing outward
     chang'd,
My death and Henry's wedding were arrang'd,

My headsman order'd, and most savage ends
Prepar'd by all my foes for all my friends.

Then at the tourney as the trumpets blew,
Henry arose like one with death to do.

One merciless fat sidelong look he gave,
From which I knew that he had dug my grave;

Then he was gone at gallop, and the fawn
Myself, was netted and the toils were drawn.

I who was England's Queen, had now to die.
That is forgotten where my ashes lie,

And where my spirit is, it is forgiven.
O living men, for pity and sweet Heaven,

Forgive what misery my thoughtlessness
Wrought ere my life was smitten with distress.

I, the White Falcon with the starry rod
Of roses, am a lesser bird with God.

I am in peace where flowers shine like stars.
The hates and angers beat against the bars

Of Love, that shuts this sunny garden close.
When the bells chime the loving overflows

Out of the garden and the angers cease;
Men's souls behold a morning star of peace

And cry: "O silvery one,
Companion of the Sun,
Mark not the thing ill-done
In the blind Night,
But mark the Life begun,
The Race still to be run,
The Hope that may be won,
Now we have light."

[HENRY VIII *rises.*]

HENRY:

And I am your King and your leader who stood
    by his strength,
You thought you could sway him or hold him,
    or rule in his name;
All three of you prosper'd, but found out your
    error at length,
All you who attempted to rule me, I made you
    all tame;
You three were but pawns in a game,
I us'd you and let you be lost.
Be glad you were worth what you cost,
But think not to vex me with blame.

I might have been priest, but my brother's death
    made me a King;
I plann'd to be worthy the office, a master indeed;
I fashion'd myself as a goldsmith who fashions a
    ring,
That none in the Kingdom but I should have
    power to lead.
  I was not a puppet nor reed,
  But a master in body and soul,

And the weeds that I could not control
I cut, as is best for a weed.

What if I found myself in earliest youth
Bound to a Spanish policy through you?
This country also has a part to play,
Not at another's bidding, but her own.
Your Spanish friends betrayed me and France
    failed me,
But England did not fail me, nor I her.

*   *   *

And you, my Prelate, who made use of England
In your Italian game, you also felt
A better player than yourself at hand,
Who wreckt the Roman scheme.

*   *   *

                And you, sweet minion,
You charmed me many hours, but did not bring
The heir the Kingdom wanted:—tales were told
Of plottings that should bring the wanted heir:

You say, false tales.
Perhaps, but they seemed likely to be true
To one who knew your nature: you were cast out
And with you all your fellows, utterly.

I found this Kingdom sway'd by foreign powers
And left her free of them: I builded up
A fleet to keep her: I uprooted all
Those states within a state which ruin states;
I made myself the head: and any head
Which had not wit to bow, I lopp'd away . . .
Good heads among them, too; better than yours.

Would I had had a stalwart son or two
From those six flimsy women whom I tried.

But that which must be is:—
                   One thing I hated:—
Disorder;—and another, want of splendour:—
Both coming from the want of resolute will
In a King's spirit. Men must think of me
As splendid in a splendid time; I did
My will as King: and ruled to greater purpose
Than any English King since Arthur's time.

K. OF ARAGON:

You had great greed
Of mastery: no other quality.

WOLSEY:

And men rejoic't that the dogs lickt your blood.

ANNE:

For all our love, that made your subjects glad.

HENRY:

A horse rolls when his saddle is taken off,
So will a land: but not while this King rode.

DESTINY:

The star is southing. The year is near to the
    height,
When you must hush till another year be perfect.
Back to your quiet, spirits; the midnight comes.

[*The* FIGURES *sink back.*]

SEEKER:

O spirits, linger: tell me one thing more.

DESTINY:

What is it that the mortal hungers for?

SEEKER:

What follows Death?

DESTINY:

Come to me, I will tell.

[SEEKER *goes up the stage. The hour strikes.*]

KATHARINE:

O April flowers,

WOLSEY:

And summer hours,

ANNE:

And autumn showers,

HENRY:

And winter cold!

227   Q

KATHARINE:

O days and hours,

WOLSEY:

And pride and powers,

ANNE:

We call them ours,

HENRY:

But cannot hold.

DESTINY:

The hour passes, the tale is told.

PENELOPE

PENELOPE
ODYSSEUS
EURYCLEIA
ATHENE

SCENE:—*A room in* PENELOPE'S *palace.* PENELOPE
seated centre on throne. ODYSSEUS *on bench right.*

PENELOPE:

O guest, I would first ask you this: who are you,
    whence you come
And what is your city, and who are your parents?

ODYSSEUS:

                                    O lady,
Not any man living upon the wide earth would
    refuse you
Your glory has reacht unto heaven, like that of
    your lord.
Would that that godlike one ruled over many
    brave men

ODYSSEUS:

Upholding the right, while his black soil grew
    barley and corn
And his trees bent with fruit and his sheep bore
    strong lambs, and the sea
Brought fish, thro' his ruling, and all of his
    commonwealth prosper'd.
But now, as I sit in your house, I would ask that
    you ask
Other things, not my kin, not my land, lest you
    o'erbrim my heart
With sorrow in calling to mind: I am one many-
    sorrowed
Nor is it right I should sit in another man's house
Moaning and mourning, for unceasing mourning
    is evil,
And one of your maids, or yourself, being angry,
    might say
That my eyes swam with tears because all of my
    wits swam with wine.

PENELOPE:

O stranger, the Deathless Ones ruined my beauty
    and body,
When the Argives went up against Troy with my
    husband Odysseus

If he could return and be minister tending my life

My glory and beauty would surely be better than
now.

Now I mourn; for the powers of evil so press me
with evil.

For the chieftains who rule in the islands, in
wooded Zakynthos,

Dulichium, Same, or neighbours in clearly seen
Ithaca,

Woo my unwilling person and scatter the wealth
of my home.

Therefore I cannot heed guests, no, nor suppliant
men,

Nor heralds, though sent from the Elders, but
pine for Odysseus,

Longing at heart, while they press on their suits,
and I plot.

First, God breathed this to my wits, that I set up
a loom

In my room, and weave cloth there, a broadcloth
of delicate kind,

I said to the suitors, "O nobles, my wooers, hear
this.

Since godlike Odysseus is dead, cease the urging
my marriage

Till the cloth has been finisht, lest all of my wool-
    work be waste.
A shroud for the hero Laertes to wrap him
    when Fate
Destroy him in length-stretching Death, lest the
    women should blame me
That he should lie shroudless that once had so
    many possessions."
So I said, and their kingly hearts trusted: then
    daily I wove
There at the great loom, but nightly unpickt it
    by torchlight.
So for three years I triumpht: and all the Achaians
    believed.
But ah, when the fourth year came round, and the
    seasons were changing
In the dying of months and fulfilment of many
    long days
Then through my house-maids, the heedless sluts,
    lo, I was caught
Unpicking, and blamed, so I finisht, unwilling,
    needs must.
Now I can neither fly marriage nor think of a wile
My parents much urge me to marry: my son is
    much shockt

(Now that he knows it) at having our living
  devoured.
For he is a man now, most able to manage a
  house,
May God give him glory . . . But even so, tell
  me your kin,
Whence you come, for you are not the son of a
  rock, nor the son
Of some oak of old stories . . .

ODYSSEUS:

O Lady, the much honoured wife
Of Odysseus, the son of Laertes, why will you
  not cease
From asking my kindred? I'll tell you: although
  it will give me
More sorrows than mine are already: for so it
  must be
To a man who has been from his country as long
  as I have now,
Much drifting through cities and peoples and
  suffering sorrows
But now I will tell what you ask me.
There is a land called Crete in the midst of the
  wine bright sea

233

Lovely and wealthy, sea-girdled, with many men
    in it,

Countless, and ninety cities, their tongues all mixt
    with each other,

Achaeans live there, and great-heart Eteocretans.

Kydonians, plume-tossing Dorians, godlike
    Pelasgi.

Among then Knossos, the mighty city where
    Minos

Was nine years King and the companion of God.

It was there that I saw King Odysseus and gave
    him my guest gifts,

When tumult of tempest had blown him on Crete
    in his going

Troyward, astray from Malea.

I, taking him up to my palace, well welcomed him
    there,

With heartiest friendship, there being much
    plenty at home.

And, to those other companions, who followed
    him there,

I gave barley-bread from the storehouse and
    brought gleaming wine

And sacrifice-oxen, that they might be happy at
    heart.

And there for twelve days the godlike Achaeans
      stayed with us.
On the thirteenth day as the wind fell, then he put
      forth.

PENELOPE:

Now truly, O stranger, I think I will prove if
      indeed
You guested my lord with his godlike companions
      abroad
There in your palace. Tell me, what clothes did
      he wear?
What was he like? Who were the comrades who
      followed him?

ODYSSEUS:

O lady, it's hard, after such length of time to
      declare
It is now twenty years since he went, setting sail
      from my country.
But yet I will tell you of how he appears in my
      heart.
The godlike Odysseus was wearing a cloak of fine
      purple
Double, and claspt with a gold brooch doubly
      groov'd.

The front of the brooch was wrought with a
   cunning work:—
A dog in his forefeet grappled a dappled fawn
That gaspt as he grippt: and all folk marvelled
   to see
How, altho' only gold-work, he throttled the
   deer,
While the deer strove with his feet, being minded
   to fly.
I notic't the glittering shirt on Odysseus' body.
Because it was like to the withered dry skin of an
   onion . . .
It had just that soft smoothness, and glossy it was
   in the sun,
A great many women stared at it.
A herald, too, followed him; one little older than
   he.
Him, too, I'll describe, what he was: he was round
   in the shoulder
Swarthy-skinned, curly-haired and had for his
   name Eurybates
Odysseus honoured him most out of all of his
   crew
Because at heart they were one.

PENELOPE:

Now, verily, stranger,
You, who were pitied before, shall now be both
    honoured
And dear, in my palace: for I, myself, gave him
    those clothes
You tell of, all folded, from out of my room; and
    I added
The glittering brooch to be precious to him; but
    alas,
Not again shall I welcome him home to his dear
    fatherland.
By a fatal decree of the gods he went into his ship
To go forth to behold Evil Troy, that is not to be
    named.

ODYSSEUS:

O honoured wife of Odysseus, son of Laertes,
Destroy not your beautiful body nor perish your
    heart
With mourning your husband. I will not in any
    way blame it
For indeed any woman would mourn for a
    husband destroyed
For the man unto whom, in her love, she bare
    children, although

237

He were worse than Odysseus, who (men say) is
    peer to the gods
But cease now from mourning and lay me up this
    in your heart.
I will tell you the utterest truth, nor deceive you
    at all.
I have heard of Odysseus returning to home; he
    is near.
Alive, in the fertile land of the men of Thesprotia.
And brings many treasures and rich as he strays
    thro' the land.
But his hollow ship and his trusty companions
    are lost
In the wine-bright sea.

Not long will the King be far from his friends and
    country:—
Nevertheless I will give you now my oath . . .
Now first may Zeus, the highest and best of gods
Bear witness here and the hearth of noble
    Odysseus
To which I have come, that this shall be all
    fulfilled.

Odysseus will come back here within this sun's cycle,
At the old moon's death and the coming-in of the new.

PENELOPE:

O guest, I would that this word might be fulfilled,
Swiftly then should you know my friendship and
      gifts
So that any meeting with you should call you
      blessed.
But this does my heart forebode and thus it shall
      be
Odysseus will not come home, nor will you find
      escort
Since there are not now such rulers within the
      palace
As Odysseus was among men—if he really was—
To welcome the honoured guests and to speed
      them forth.

[She goes over to the left.]

But, handmaidens, wash this guest's feet and
      prepare him a bed
Pallet and mantles and glittering rugs, that he
      come
Warmly and snugly to golden-throned Morning
      to-morrow.

And then very early at dawn you must bathe and
    anoint him
So that he dine with Telemachus there in the hall,
And it shall be the worse for the one of the
    wooers
Who injures this man, *his* business shall not
    thrive
However he rage.
              For how would you learn, O guest,
That I am wiser and shrewder than other women
If I let you dine in the hall, ill-clad, sun-beaten?

ODYSSEUS:

O honoured wife of Odysseus, Laertes' son,
Mantles and glittering rugs have been hateful to
    me,
Since first I drew away from the snowy mountains
Of Crete, out-bound in the long-oared ship.
                        I'll lie
As formerly in the sleepless nights I stretcht,
Ay, many a night, in a bed not like a bed
Stretcht, to await the well-throned glittering
    morning.
And washing of feet is no longer the joy of my
    heart.

Nor shall one of the women now servants here in
    your house
Touch my foot, save some old dame here of old
Trusty of heart, who has borne such grief
    as I.
I would not grudge such an one to touch my feet.

PENELOPE:

Dear guest, not yet has any such wise man come
To my house, of all dear guests out of distant
    lands,
To speak such eloquent right in all that he
    says.
I have an old servant here who is wise at heart
Who nursed and fostered yonder ill-fated man
And carried him in her arms when his mother
    bare him.
She shall wash your feet, although she is feeble
    now.

[PENELOPE *claps her hands.*]

But come now, rise now, wise hearted Eurycleia,
And wash one like to your lord . . .
                  for the feet and hands

Of Odysseus now will be even as these of his.
For men among evils swiftly grow old.

EURYCLEIA:

Alas!
Woe's me, child, unable to help you, surely our
    God
Loathed you above all mortals although you were
    righteous
For never has mortal yet burnt so many thighs
Or offerings pickt, to God Delighting in
    Thunder,
As you once gave with prayer that yourself might
    come
To a smooth old age and rear your glorious son.
Now God has taken from you all day of returning.

[EURYCLEIA *now turns to* ODYSSEUS' *self, the
Stranger.* PENELOPE *goes off left.*]

And perhaps the women are mocking Odysseus
    now
In a far-off stranger land in a famous house
As the shameless sluts all mock at your presence
    here.

It is to avoid their outrage and many insults
That you will not let them bathe your feet.
Icarius' daughter, the prudent Penelope
Has ordered me, who am not unwilling, to bathe
     them
For Penelope's sake and also because of yours.
Since my heart is moved within me with pity for
     you.
But come now, 'tend to the word that I shall
     speak.
Many much-suffering strangers have drifted
     hither,
But I say, I have not yet seen one so much like
As you, to Odysseus, body and voice and feet.

ODYSSEUS:

So all men say, who have seen us both with
     eyes,
That we're very much like each other, as now you
     notice.

[EURYCLEIA *kneels to the washing, the curtain is*
     drawn. ATHENE *goes rapidly to the centre stage*
     as the curtain closes behind her.]

Now Odysseus sat turned from the hearth
Then swiftly he turned to the darkness, he feared
    in his heart
Lest handling his scar she might know it, and
    facts become clear.
She went to her master to bathe him and straight-
    way she knew
The wound which the boar had once dealt him
    with white tusk of old.
When the early-born rose-fingered Dawn shone,
He went out to hunt with the hounds and
    Autolycus' sons.
Up the steep, forest-garmented mountain Par-
    nassus, he went
And swiftly came up to the windy ravines as the
    Sun
From the soft-flowing deep-flowing Ocean
    struck bright on the fields.
Then the hunters went into a glen, and in front
    of them went
The hounds, on a scent, and behind them Auto-
    lycus' sons,
And with them the godlike Odysseus went close
    to the hounds

Poising a long-shadowed spear. There a mighty
    boar lay
In a harbour so tangled that neither the might of
    wet winds
Might blow through its cover, nor bright Sun
    beat through it with rays
Nor thunderstorm pierce it, but masses of many
    dead leaves lay.
Then the noise of the feet of the men and the dogs
    reached the boar
As they came, setting on, and he leapt out in
    front of his lair
Well bristling his hackles and gleaming with
    flame in his eyes,
And stood up against them, and first of them all
    King Odysseus,
Charged, lifting long spear in grapple intending
    to smite.
And rushing, the wild boar forestalled him and
    struck above knee,
Ripping it sideways and tearing much flesh with
    his tusk,
Not reaching the bone of the man. And
    Odysseus smote him
Home, in right shoulder, the point of the bright
    spear went through.

And he fell in the dust with a scream and his life
    fluttered out.
Then the dear sons of Autolycus brittled the boar
And bandaged the gash of the noble, godlike
    Odysseus
Staunching the black blood with song: then they
    straightway returned
Back to Autolycus' palace, and there they well
    healed him,
Giving him glorious gifts, and speedily sent him
To Ithaca home in love, glad hosts, glad guest.

[*Here* ATHENE *comes to lower stage, extreme left.*]

Now Eurycleia, seeing the scar, at once
Knew that she toucht Odysseus' self and straight
Her joy and grief took hold of her wits, her eyes
Filled with tears, and her clear voice checked, as
    she said:

[*Here* ATHENE *goes off the stage, the curtain is
    drawn and displays* EURYCLEIA *kneeling at*
    ODYSSEUS' *feet, touching his chin as a suppliant.*]

EURYCLEIA:

You are Odysseus' self, dear child, and I did not
    know

Before, until I had handled my Lord all over.

[ODYSSEUS *grips her throat with his right hand and draws her to him with his left.*]

ODYSSEUS:

Nurse, why do you wish to destroy me?—You, too, who once nurst me
On your own breast—now, when after enduring much woe,
I come, in the twentieth year, to my father land?
But since you have known me, since God has put this in your mind,
Silence, lest any one else in the hall spy me out.
Or I tell you this, and it will be brought to fulfilment,
If God subdues these excellent wooers to me
I will not spare you, not though you be my nurse
When I kill the other women who serve in my halls.

EURYCLEIA:

My child, what word has crosst the hedge of your teeth?
You know how my mind is firm and not to be won.

I'll stand as stark as a stone or steel; and I tell you
(You keep it well in your heart) that if God
    should grant
That you subdue these excellent wooers, I'll tell
    you
Which of the women dishonour you, which are
    guiltless.

ODYSSEUS:

Nurse, why do you speak of these, when there is
    not need?
I'll notice them well myself and mark each one.
You hold to a silent mind and trust to the gods.

[EURYCLEIA *goes off,* left front: ODYSSEUS *covers*
    his scar: PENELOPE *enters,* left back.]

PENELOPE:

Stranger, I yet must ask you one little thing.
Swiftly the hour for untroubled resting is coming
To him whom the sweet sleep takes, however
    much harrasst.
But to me God gives measureless sorrow, for
    daylong I mourn,

Weeping, appointing the tasks of the maids in the
    house
Yet when the night comes, and all sleep, I am
    there in my bed
And sharp sorrows thronging about me are thick
    at my heart,
Rousing my sorrowing like as the daughter of
    Pandarus
The olive-green singer, sweet singing in new-
    comen spring
Percht in the thick leaves of trees, often altering
    mode
Pours many-toned song in lamenting her child,
    her dear Itylus,
(Son of Zethus, the prince) whom she slew with
    the bronze through mistake.
So hither and thither my mind is tormented
    asunder,
Whether to stay with my son and guard all things
    unchanged,
My treasures, my house-folk, my high-rooft
    great palace, respecting
My vows to my husband, and also the voice of
    the people,
Or go with the best of the Greeks wooing here in
    the hall?

While my son was a child and a light-heart, I
    could not well marry
Nor go from the house of my husband, but now
    he is grown
And come to the measure of manhood, and now
    he implores me
To go from this house, being vext for his wealth,
    which the wooers
Devour together.
But come, now, and hark to my dream and inter-
    pret it to me.

I keep twenty geese at the farm, eating grain
    from the pool,
I am happy to see them. Now out of the moun-
    tain there came
A great crook-beakt eagle that struck on their
    necks and killed all.
They lay heapt in hall while he lifted aloft
    through bright air.
And I cried and made clamour although it was
    only a dream.
And the women of Greece with the beautiful hair
    gathered round me
To my pitiful cry that the eagle had slaughtered
    my geese.

But the eagle came back and was percht on an
    outjutting cornice.
And ending my weeping he spoke with the voice
    of a man.

"Courage, o daughter of far-famed Icarius,
    listen . . .
This is no dream but the truth: you shall see it
    fulfilled.
The geese are the wooers, and I was the eagle but
    now.
But *now* am your husband returned who will
    bring shameful death
On all of the wooers." So said he. Then sweet
    sleep release me
And I saw all the geese in the hall eating corn
    from the bin
Where they formerly were.

ODYSSEUS:

        O lady, man cannot interpret
Your dream, wresting meanings awry, since
    Odysseus himself
Shows how he means to fulfil it: Death comes to
    the wooers
To all of them, all; not a man shall escape death
    and doom.

PENELOPE:

Stranger, a dream and the judging a dream are
    both baffling.

Nor are all dreams fulfilled among men.

There are two gates of powerless dreams, one of
    horn, one of ivory,

Those which come through the ivory gate, cheat
    the hope, bearing nothings;

Those which come through the doors of wrought
    horn, they are truly fulfilled

To the mortal who sees them; but my dream, I
    think, came not thence.

Good to me, to myself, and my son were it so.
    I say thus: mind it well.

Even now is the evil dawn breaking that sweeps
    me away

From the house of Odysseus, for now I must set
    up a contest

With the axes Odysseus was used to set up in his
    halls

Like the oak blocks of keels, twelve in all; he
    would stand far apart

And hurtle an arrow through all; this I'll set for
    the wooers.

He who most easily strings my lord's bow with
    his hands
And shoots through the rings of twelve axes, I'll
    follow that man
I'll abandon this house of my marriage, this
    beautiful house
All full of good living . . .
I think I shall think of it always, ay, even in
    dreams.

ODYSSEUS:

O Lady, the wife of Odysseus, the son of
    Laertes,
Delay not this contest, because many-crafted
    Odysseus
Will be here before these who fondle the well-
    polisht bow
Shall string it with sinew and hurtle a shaft
    through the iron.

PENELOPE:

O guest, if you would but sit thus in my halls
    giving comfort
Beside me, sleep would not be laid on my eyelids
    at all.

But men may not always be sleepless; the Deathless have made
A Fate for each thing among men on the corn-
giving world
I shall go to my high upper room and there lay
me to bed
All made with my sorrows and soiled with my
weeping since he,
Odysseus went forth to see Evil Troy not to be
named.
There I shall rest; but yourself will lie here in the
house,
Either stretcht on the ground, or let some set a
bed for you here.

[PENELOPE *goes off, left, down stage.* ODYSSEUS
*spreads mats on the ground as though for his bed.
He goes up right, and listens.*]

ODYSSEUS:

Those women go out from the house: they are
bound for the Wooers . . .
Shall I rush out and kill them, each one? Shall I
leave them to love
Those proud ones this last latest time? For I rage
at their evil . . .

But bear it, my heart, you have borne a more
    dog-like thing once,
In the day when the uncheckt mad Cyclops
    devoured my mates,
You bore it, till cunning had led you safe out of
    the cave
Where you reckoned to die . . .

[ATHENE *appears above.*]

ATHENE:

Why are you watching, most luckless of all men
    alive?
This is your palace, your wife is within in the
    house,
And your son, such a captain as any would wish
    for a son.

ODYSSEUS:

Yes, all of these things are the truth, Goddess;
    rightly you speak,
But my heart in my bosom debates, how to put
    out my hands
On these shameless ones, being but one, and
    themselves always many.

255

But still more I think in my heart. If by God's
    help and yours
I kill them, how 'scape the Avengers? Advise
    and command.

ATHENE:

O doubter, men trust in a sorrier comrade than I,
In a mortal, who knows no such counsel; but I
    am a God
Who will faithfully guard you in all of your
    troubles whatever.
I tell you this plainly, should fifty pickt squadrons
    of men
Surround us, all minded to kill us, yet still you
    should win
And drive off their cattle and flocks. But let sleep
    take you now.
It is pain to guard all night awake. You shall
    soon rise from troubles.

[*She pours slumber upon* ODYSSEUS: *he sleeps.*]